The Scandal of Psychotherapy

The Scandal of Psychotherapy

A Guide to Resolving the Tensions between Faith and Counseling

Clinton W. McLemore

Tyndale House Publishers, Inc.   Wheaton, Illinois

The author gratefully acknowledges permission to reprint passages from the following previously published material:

Argus Communications, excerpt from *He Touched Me: My Pilgrimage of Prayer,* by John Powell. Copyright © 1974 by Argus Communications. Used by permission.

William B. Eerdmans Publishing Co., excerpts from "Pierre Teilhard de Chardin," by Richard Acworth and from "Paul Tillich," by Kenneth Hamilton, both appearing in *Creative Minds in Contemporary Theology,* second edition, edited by Philip Edgcumbe Hughes. Copyright © 1969 by William B. Eerdmans. Used by permission. Also, from *A Theology of the New Testament,* by George Eldon Ladd. Copyright © 1974 by William B. Eerdmans. Used by permission.

Macmillan Publishing Co., excerpt from *Screwtape Letters,* by C. S. Lewis. Copyright © 1942 by C. S. Lewis. Used by permission.

McGraw-Hill Book Company, excerpt from *To Love Again: A Psychiatrist's Search for Love,* by Norman Garbo. Copyright © 1977 by Norman Garbo. Used by permission of McGraw-Hill Book Company.

Simon & Schuster, Publishers, excerpt from *A History of Western Philosophy,* by Bertrand Russell. Copyright © 1945 by Bertrand Russell. Used by permission of Simon & Schuster.

First printing, March 1982
Library of Congress Catalog Card Number 81-84288
ISBN 0-8423-5853-6, cloth
ISBN 0-8423-5852-8, paper
Printed in the United States of America

*To my beloved family of the
First Presbyterian Church of Hollywood,
for so often showing me God's love,
and for having the generosity and foresight
to share with others across the land
the Good News of Jesus Christ.*

CONTENTS

FOREWORD

I believe we are living in one of the most exciting times since Pentecost. The penetrating power of the Holy Spirit, a new emphasis on biblical preaching, and the growing appreciation of the psychological dynamics of human personality are bringing about a profound renaissance. Local congregations are discovering what it means to be a laboratory of new life. Religious people are being liberated to experience fresh grace. An authentic marriage of biblical theology and Christian psychology has enabled clergy, church officers, and members to live the adventure of the abundant life. Increasingly, local churches are healing communities in which the deepest inner needs of people are being exposed and healed.

There is a great difference between the God of our previous experience and our continuing experience of God. It is possible to allow our initial, introductory experience of God to hinder our continued growth as persons. There is nothing more foolish than answers to unasked questions or the conceptual proclamation of the gospel, both of which bypass the gut issues and raw nerves inside people. Equally so, there is nothing more powerful than the vulnerable, personally illustrated, Holy Spirit-empowered preaching and teaching of the

Scriptures in the ambience of an honest, open fellowship.

The reason that previously dull churches are becoming dynamic is that we as Christians are beginning to take seriously the disturbing memories which restrict our freedom, the personality patterns which defeat us, and the relational tensions which make us defensive. Sanctification, the dynamic process of experiencing the character transplant of Christ into our total being, must follow conversion. There is a fresh excitement in church people who are discovering Christ's healing in the deepest recesses of their personalities. They bring a vitality and viability to the local congregation as well as contagious witness in the world. Little can happen *through* us which is not happening *to* us. In the past, far too little happened in congregations to help people experience the Lord's unconditional love, to enable them to love themselves creatively and others courageously. Until Christ is allowed to love us profoundly, confronting us with the real persons we are, we will limp through life.

God's gift of Christian psychology to the church has made us appreciate the hidden recesses of our natures and the healing that can be accomplished in Christ. Christ is all or not at all. To begin the Christian life is to give as much of ourselves as we know to as much of him as we have experienced. But growth in the Christian life is an ever-increasing understanding of ourselves which must be given to his forgiveness and repatterning power.

We are promised a new creation, that we will become new creatures in whom the old passes away and the new comes. This is the ministry of the Holy Spirit. But we've all known in ourselves, and observed in others, the sapping drain of creative energies caused by fear, anxiety, and frustration. We bring into the new life all that has happened to and around us in our growing years. Unresolved hurts dominate our responses and reactions. Each self-discovery leads to deeper grace. Once we have been reconciled to God, our great need is to be reconciled to the inner person who lives in our skin. As the Lord heals the past which inevitably invades our present effectiveness, we can be set free to be warm, gracious, accepting people. We need not continue the duality of dishonesty—the external projection of pity and the inner cauldron of anger and hurting memories. Christian psychology can help us do that.

We've all suffered at the hands of Christians whose inner tensions have caused continual conflict, broken relationships, and disruption of the fellowship. And we are all in touch with Christians whose need for psychological healing causes depression and inability to function creatively, or those who find deep relationships difficult, if not impossible. We wring our hands in consternation or smack our lips in criticism, asking, "Why can't they be more Christian?" Then in more tender moments we ask, "How did they get that way?" But in times of personal honesty we realize our own need for healing. Christian psychology can help us—the pain of the past can be healed and we can become new creatures in every facet of our being and our relationships. The Lord is never finished with us. That's why he gave the church the gift of Christian psychologists and the insights of modern psychology—to help us understand and process the memory factors which determine who we are and what we do. The impact of Christian psychology upon the contemporary renaissance of the church is profound. It has recalled us to people and their needs as our primary agenda and has dared to assert again that human nature can be changed.

When Christian psychology is accepted as a friend rather than an enemy, pastors are able to lead their congregations in the renaissance of remedial counseling. The parishes I observe which are coming alive are being led by men and women who are experiencing healing in their own lives. They have studied not only the dynamics of psychology in their theological education, but have opened themselves to honest self-evaluation. Many have received counseling or psychotherapy; others are part of support groups in which they are given freedom to be open about what's happening to and around them. Preaching is not just preparing a biblical exposition and delivering it. Preaching means allowing the Lord to prepare the preacher, and then the exposition comes alive with vulnerability and incisive illustration. Realized truth, experienced not only conceptually but experientially and relationally, results in the vibrant communication of the gospel. Our ongoing remedial, psychological growth also has its impact on the total congregational life. Church officers are challenged by the freedom and flexibility of the pastor. An exciting thing happens to a church when its officers are led into deep personal growth and accepting fellowship. A congregation will move only as far as the officers have experienced the healing of the gospel. When that adventure begins, and officers are astounded with the serendipities of the Lord's intervention in their personal lives, a new daring emerges in the church's program. The real needs of people become the focus for the teaching and fellowship programs of the church.

The Christian psychologist becomes a great resource in this renaissance. He can be a vital resource not only as one to whom the pastor can refer people for help, but also as a confidant in the maintenance of his or her own psychological health in the midst of the pressures and demands of parish life. In the matter of referrals, no pastor should be expected to do *long-range* psycho-logical counseling. He usually has neither the time nor the training. A creative relationship with a number of Christian psychologists multiplies the pastor's ministry.

One of the most creative contributions of the psychologist to the pastor is help in the development of a psychologically healthy congregational life. With the trained psychologist, the pastor can ask the hard questions about what's coming through his ministry: if there is a gracious ambience in church groups and programs in which people can grow, and the extent to which guilt or legalism is crippling relationships.

This may be a long leap for some church leaders because of personal defensiveness or the questions they may have about some of the more eccentric expressions of the mental health profession. Not all psychology is healing or helpful. Radical expressions of some schools of thought in psychology are not compatible with the Christian faith. How can Christians know what is authentic? How can they make their way through the labyrinth of various theories? How can an individual select a competent psychologist to help him clear away a path through the thicket of his fears and repressions in order to grow as a person? How can a church leader find help for his own and his congregation's healing? These questions make this book you are about to read so crucial and strategic.

Dr. Clinton W. McLemore's *The Scandal of Psychotherapy* concerns the relationship of Christianity and psychology. This stunning book by one of America's leading Christian psychologists is a unique combination of the author's scholarship, his in-depth experience as an outstanding psychotherapist, and his disarming, if not daring, honesty about what it means to be whole in Christ. Here is a benchmark contribution to the dialogue between theology and psychology. It is superbly written, carefully documented, and vividly illustrative. But most important of all, the reader is invited inside the mind of a person who has dared to stand in the gap that has been excavated by suspicions and misunderstandings between theologians and psychologists and has integrated and absorbed the valuable contributions of both disciplines.

The thing which makes the book so valuable is that Dr. McLemore is a top-rate scholar, committed Christian, faithful churchman, and very gifted psychotherapist. There is an autobiographical thread which knits the research, case histories, and personal illustrations together into a readable and stimulating book. As his pastor and friend, I know him as a man in Christ with an incessant quest to know himself and Christ better and to communicate grace to others. The impact of his counseling, teaching, and influence on our congregation is immense. He is a beloved teacher in the Fuller Graduate School of Psychology and a frontiersman breaking ground with new thought and insight. Here is an original thinker who allows the reader to examine the shavings as well as the finished carving of his ideas, as he whittles and hones them toward perfection, toward art and a clarity of expression.

As with any great book, there are aspects with which the reader wants to grapple and ideas to question further. There were times when I said to myself as a theologian and pastor, "I really want to talk with Clinton about that!" One area which raised questions and concerns in my mind was the chapter on the Law and health, and the subsequent review paragraphs on the subject in the final chapter. I had to remind myself that the author is writing from the standpoint of a psychotherapist who seeks to work with people in a nonjudgmental way, many of whom have broken God's Law. The author has raised a crucial and complicated question about whether breaking the Law can ever yield good. My belief is that it does not. The salient thing is whether we are to look retrospectively or prospectively on the possibility. In reflection with a patient, a psychologist may be able to discern and help him or her realize deeper healing which has come through the failure and subsequent experience of grace. As you will see throughout the book, Dr. McLemore is committed to Christian morality and the Decalogue and does not advocate license in any way. In conversation with him about this matter prior to my writing this foreword, I brought into question the responsibility of the Christian psychologist as advocate in matters of the Law and morality. His response was a forceful assertion of his own commitment to the Law, his desire to communicate that to his patients, and also his dedication to assist patients in dealing with their brash or subtle infringements of God's Law.

At issue is Paul's statement to the Romans, "What shall we say then? Shall we continue in sin that grace may abound? Certainly not!" (Romans 6:1, 2). To encourage or tacitly applaud breaking the Law so that a person could come to a deeper breakthrough of grace, would be to add to the reservoir of distressed conscience and guilt. Surely God can and will find other ways of breaking the pride of a prig. A physician would not induce physical illness to cure the arrogance of a person about always being healthy.

Jesus Christ came not to destroy but to fulfill the Law. Through him we become free to obey the Ten Commandments, not as an end in themselves, but as God's clearly delineated relational righteousness with him, ourselves, and others. I would affirm the author's clear statement on page 74, " . . . I do not choose to encourage violations of the moral Law, even if such violations are likely to produce temporal psychological benefits."

All this puts into sharp focus the need for partnership of the church and Christian psychology. In the past, the church has communicated more Law than grace. The result was far too little of either. The healing of persons calls us to engage them in an authentic encounter with God which issues in healthy freedom *and* obedience. For this awesome calling to the church as a healing community, psychologists and church leaders desperately need each other.

This excellent book will engage you in a challenging dialogue with the author. He will make you think, reflect on your own spiritual and psychological healing, and wonder whether what Christ has done in this man's life has happened to you. In point of fact, it can and may.

Lloyd John Ogilvie

PREFACE

Any author's ideas, however original they may seem, come from combinations and refinements of others' ideas—new books come from old conversations!

Conversations, in the broadest sense, take various forms. There are brisk dialogues over coffee, scholarly lectures, and even the intimate sense of communication that can emerge from reading stimulating books. Such conversations are essential to the development of a writer's work. There is just no such thing as a solitary scholar or, for that matter, a truly self-educated person.

Many people contributed in one way or another to my fund of ideas and consequently to the writing of this book. Here I would like to thank those from whom I have learned the most and who, therefore, have had the most to do with *The Scandal of Psychotherapy.*

In the years that I have taught at Fuller Theological Seminary, I have had the opportunity to take theology courses from James Bradley, Geoffrey Bromiley, James Daane, Jack Rogers, and Lewis Smedes. As with the other persons I will cite, I do not want to imply that anyone of them would unreservedly endorse what I have written. Nevertheless, these people have had a strong impact on me.

The theologian most directly associated with this book

is Paul Jewett, insofar as I originally wrote down the ideas upon which this book is based for a course we taught together. I am grateful for his encouragement and for his unending willingness to help me understand theological issues. Colin Brown, another specialist in systematic theology at Fuller, has also been generous with his time and expertise.

I owe a particular debt to three philosophers who over the years have spent much time and energy to educate a "behavioral scientist" in the methods and materials of their discipline. Nearly two decades ago, William Devlin, a college classmate, cultivated my love for speculative questions. I caught his enthusiasm for clear thinking as well as his dis-ease over intellectual sloppiness, and the affliction has remained with me ever since!

Paul Sharkey, with whom I used to work but who now teaches at the University of Southern Mississippi, has helped me struggle through philosophic questions for the better part of a decade. Paul's personal graciousness, special competence in epistemology and in the philosophy of science, and interest in medical-psychological issues have always made it easy for us to talk.

My debt to Geddes MacGregor, Emeritus Distinguished Professor of Philosophy at the University of Southern California, is enormous. For years, this close friend and I have gotten together regularly to chat, with the happy consequence that I have had the privilege of spending many hours in the presence of one of the greatest living philosophers of religion. Moreover, he read the manuscript for this book prior to my final revisions and gave me a wealth of helpful advice, both technical and conceptual. The inadequacies that remain are there only because in certain places I have chosen, perhaps stubbornly, to go my own way.

Two other friends, who by coincidence share the same last name, also critiqued the manuscript. William McCormick made detailed and scholarly comments on an early draft. Kathy McCormick did the same for a later draft. Their extensive comments concerning both style and content reflected painstaking labors of love, for which I am much indebted.

The person who has contributed most to my spiritual development is Dan Ballinger. Many years ago, we began a deep friendship that has continued to spawn theological reflection. On several occasions (when we were younger!) we talked from sunset to sunrise, when dawn brought with it the reminder that we had forfeited another night's sleep to discuss ideas. Many of these ideas had to do with the relationship between psychology and theology.

Bryant Crouse, a clinical psychologist with singular gifts whom I have known since prep school, has always encouraged me to write books. When this book was no more than a vague notion of a possible project, he urged me to carry it through. For this, and his rich friendship, I am thankful.

Several people gave me editorial reactions and suggestions on some or all of the manuscript. Of special help were Audrey Beslow, Jo Gifford, Curtis Helms, Eric Jacobson, Keith McMullen, Fritz Ridenour, Linda Smith, Anna Stepp, Sam Southard, Val Toms, and Anne Wheeler. My wife Alicia's comments were particularly helpful.

Some people indirectly but nonetheless importantly influenced the content of this volume by showing me living examples of God at work in the world. Their lives, which have repeatedly encouraged me in the Christian faith, are expressions of Christ's presence in the twentieth century. At the risk of embarrassing them, I list them here: Larry Burge, Peter Esser, John Fantuzzo, Frank Grob, Phyllis Hart, Paul Hedwall, James Long, Wayne Marshall, Robert Munger, Alan Stones, and Fred Woodbury. I express special appreciation for support to the men in my fellowship group: Roger Chastain, Andrew Gifford, Richard Kaufmann, Norman Nelson, Rick Sholl, and Robert Toms.

Early drafts of the book were typed by my former secretary, Margot Day. Her competence and professional dedication were a huge blessing to me. My present secretary, Bert Jacklitch, has carried on in Margot's tradition. She is bright, efficient, thoroughly responsible, and a total delight to work with. Another Fuller secretary, Donna Viselli, has helped me with key tasks.

I express, once again, my love and appreciation to my mother, Clara. The emotional nurturance she gave me as a young child, coupled with her belief in my abilities, has played a large part in my creative work. I also express love and appreciation to my wife's parents, Carlos and Alicia Horacio, who have given to me and my family great gifts of many kinds.

Finally, I thank Lloyd John Ogilvie, senior pastor of the First Presbyterian Church of Hollywood, for his vitally important ministry in my life and in the lives of others all across the country. He and his associates, in particular; Paul Cedar; Rob Norris, and Ralph Osborne, have taught me much about Jesus.

Clinton McLemore

A READER'S GUIDE

This book is addressed to anyone who is seriously interested in understanding the relationship between modern psychological helping methods and the Christian faith. In writing it, I have had in mind several groups of readers: persons currently in, or about to enter, psychotherapy; mental health professionals, including psychiatrists, psychologists, social workers, marriage and family therapists, psychiatric nurses, and paraprofessional counselors; pastoral counselors who, along with family physicians, are consulted far more readily than other professionals*; seminary students, who often feel confused and bewildered by the challenge of fitting together what they learn in their counseling and theology courses; and, finally, people who are just intellectually curious about what Christianity and psychotherapy have to do with each other.

Writing for such a large audience has its pitfalls. Specifically, the writer runs the risk of losing some readers "here" and other readers "there." A chapter that might prove highly stimulating to a practicing psychotherapist could seem, to the casual reader, as just so much academic nitpicking—much ado about nothing. Conversely, chapters that might be very helpful to a layperson who is searching for a good therapist could be little more than a review to the sophisticated mental health expert. In the face of this challenge, what is a writer to do?

I have chosen to write what I believe is a solid book, but to write it in a style that is easy to read. There is no way to do justice to our subject without some technical discussion. At the same time, technical discussions that are dry and uninteresting are often of little value. The best technical discussions of all are those that can hardly be recognized as such! Based on the positive responses I have gotten to the manuscript in typed form, I am hopeful that large numbers of people will find this book both informative and readable.

Chapter 1 suggests that psychologists and theologians urgently need to talk more with each other, and it gives some reasons why this is so. Chapter 2 has to do with the nature of religious knowledge and considers the importance of basic assumptions. Chapter 3 treats the relationship between spiritual and psychological healing. Chapter 4 shows how eternal well-being and feeling good in the present may not always be the same thing. Chapter 5 concerns the healing work of the Holy Spirit. Chapter 6 highlights how the Christian therapist is potentially caught between the church and the state. Chapter 7 outlines the extent to which Scripture reveals the intricate everyday workings of human personality. Chapter 8 illustrates the need for therapists to take seriously the nature of the human spirit. Chapters 9 and 10 critique various popular forms of psychological help, from both clinical and theological points of view. Chapter 11 is highly personal and presents my own experiences as a therapy client. Finally, chapter 12 reviews the basic arguments presented in the book.

Despite the obvious fact that different chapters from any book will appeal to different readers, all good books are constructed around a central theme. The pivotal idea here is that unbelievers have only one perspective from which to view life—the temporal—while Christians have two—the temporal and the eternal. We will explore how these two perspectives relate to each other and what this has to do with the nature of psychotherapy.

---

*See my *Clergyman's Psychological Handbook: Clinical Information for Pastoral Counseling* (Grand Rapids: William B. Eerdmans, 1974).

INTRODUCTION

The English word "scandal" comes from the Greek word
skandalon, which means "stumbling block" or "offense."
If many people are scandalized by the notion of
consulting a psychotherapist, then Christians are doubly
offended by such an idea. First, it is assumed that
Christians should be psychologically perfect. A Christian
should not need to consult a mental health professional,
the thinking goes; when Christians do, they are often
thought to lack faith. Second, Christians tend to perceive
psychotherapy as a kind of "new religion." To see a
therapist seems to some a rejection of the church, or
worse, a turning away from Christ. To what degree are
these feelings legitimate?

I have been a Christian for about twenty years.
Coming to believe in Christ turned my life upside down
—or was it right side up? Life *consciously* took on a
transcendent dimension for me. The world has seemed
different ever since. My values have changed, and I
believe that I am now related to God in a way I never
was before. He is my Father, I am his child, and we
have a conversational and, at times, even a negotiational
relationship. Moreover, I have experienced God *in* my
life and I have seen him work in the lives of many
other people. Having come to know the reality of his

presence and power, I cannot trivialize or ignore the spiritual. Life in Christ involves the supernatural, and I must reckon with this in my thinking and in my practice as a psychologist.

I have been a clinical psychologist for almost as long as I have been a Christian. My professional work includes teaching, research, and writing. Most important of all, however, it involves me in the lives of hurting people. Many of these people I have been able to help. They feel understood, experience life in a new and deeper way, learn better procedures for coping with stress, get free of debilitating anxiety and immobilizing depression, and so forth. Any competent therapist could list similar accomplishments. The question in all of this is: How does psychotherapy relate to historic Christianity?

We will take a careful look at the relationship between transformation in Christ and psychotherapeutic healing. Of special interest to us will be clinical cases in which spiritual and psychological well-being *seem* to be at odds. We will consider the ethics of the therapist introducing discussions of Jesus Christ into the treatment process—how much is the Christian therapist caught between the mandates and expectations of a "secular state" on the one hand, and the dictates of Christian conscience on the other? We will also ask some other questions. To what extent does the Bible tell the therapist how to provide help to troubled persons? What is the significance of the human spirit in therapy? Do such popular forms of psychological help as behavior therapy, client-centered counseling, and psychoanalysis carry with them theological implications?

For many questions, I will not, and indeed cannot, supply final answers. I will merely point out some of the critical issues, along with the consequences of answering the questions in particular ways. In no instance will I dilute or alter what I understand to be the Christian message in order to wiggle out of a troubling dilemma. Many of the questions we will address seem to defy simple answers. They are just too multifaceted. In many cases, the most we can probably do is to frame the question clearly. Still, asking a good question is sometimes an important step in finding an answer.

Along with philosophers of science, we must have the intellectual integrity to acknowledge that any given "fact pattern" is open to an infinite number of interpretations. The hope of logically proving the validity of Christianity is, therefore, generally misguided. What is evidence for belief to the Christian may be evidence for unbelief to the atheist. Nevertheless, conflicts between psychology and theology are often more apparent than real. When the conflicts *are* real, they exist usually between some point of Christian doctrine and some philosophical assertion that is being incorrectly represented as "science."

The day has passed when a psychotherapist could convincingly claim to be philosophically neutral. Regardless of theoretical orientation, all therapists communicate, in subtle or not-so-subtle ways, metaphysical and ethical beliefs to their clients. Because the psychotherapy patient ordinarily comes for treatment in a demoralized condition and thus looks to the mental health professional for all sorts of guidance, the therapist is thrust into a position of extraordinary power. More often than not, people come to mental health experts precisely because they want to be persuaded to see things differently, to hold more functional attitudes and beliefs, to think better, to feel better, and so on. The patient, therefore, is usually a trusting seeker who, out of need, pushes the therapist into the role of sagacious guide or omniscient guru.

Our primary question has to do with the relationship between psychology and theology. The two seem to struggle for control over the individual person. Both claim to be true: psychology by way of the scientific method; theology by virtue of divine revelation. But if we are to explore this conflict successfully, we must be intellectually honest. Psychologists must admit that much of psychology, for all its scientific rigor, derives from metaphysical assumptions and standards which are set arbitrarily and culturally. Theologians must admit that, ultimately, Christianity cannot be logically proved, but must be taken (at least in part) by faith. In both disciplines—psychology and theology—any set of facts, circumstances, or situations (in other words, any "fact pattern") is subject to a variety of interpretations. Quite simply, there is a lot we do not know, a lot we cannot explain with certainty. Often, when there appears to be a conflict between psychology and theology, it is really just one or the other asserting something dogmatically, something which it does not have the authority to proclaim.

Psychological researchers have long realized that the definition of normality itself is, to a large extent, arbitrary and culturally conditioned. While no one would argue that definitions of mental health are completely capricious (a patient claiming to be Napoleon Bonaparte, or someone who visits with "little green men" every day, is likely to be thought of by most people as deviant), still, anthropologists have documented the striking degree to which notions of psychological well-being are culturally relative.

To cite just two examples, Reno Fortune[1] illustrated how the Dobuan islanders operate within a generalized paranoid belief system, and how in that culture to do otherwise would seem to be pathological! Another example would be the World War II Nazis, who deemed genocide to be in the service of advancing the welfare of the human race.

Put these two things together—the psychotherapist's inescapable role as philosopher-sage and the arbitrary nature of the goals of psychotherapy—and it must be conceded that psychotherapy is more art than science and more intimately related to the function of the shaman than to that of, say, the physical chemist or the neurosurgeon.

Many Christian therapists still merrily skip along in the naive belief that they can endlessly avoid coming to terms with the tensions between Christian beliefs and atheistically conditioned views of psychotherapy. As I will show in this book, psychotherapy need not be practiced from an anti-theistic position but, in fact, it often is. To argue for the total independence of the theological and the psychological is to divorce horizontal (immanent) reality from vertical (transcendent) reality. It is to argue either that psychological practice is completely scientific—which is absurd—or that psychotherapy is simply a means of common grace and that the spiritual needs of the patient should be met only by those resources equally available to the atheist and the Christian! Such a view allows secular society too much control over how psychotherapy is best defined and conducted.

Christian psychotherapists have at their disposal a very special resource—the activity of the Holy Spirit. The Spirit, according to the Christian view, can operate on, and through, the personality of the therapist. This means, in ideal practice, that the Christian psychotherapist *will* influence the patient to conform to the image of Christ. Of course, such influence should consist not of weighing patients down with the Law but rather of lifting them up with the grace of Jesus. Just as non-Christian mental health practitioners cannot credibly argue that they have no philosophic influence over their patients, Christian therapists must face up to the clear reality that they, too, are in the influencing business. To be sure, the expert conduct of psychotherapy by anyone, Christian or not, involves more than persuasion. A lot of therapy *is* more clinically technical than philosophically persuasive. But the latter can rarely if ever be entirely avoided, nor should it be. As the eminent psychiatrist Jerome Frank pointed out years ago,[2] healing and persuasion often march along together.

It is time for Christians in the mental health professions to confront their spiritual responsibilities to patients and to recognize the true nature of what they do. While I do not agree that psychotherapy can be reduced simply to one more form of "disciple-making," enhancing the faith-walk of Christian clients must surely be among the Christian therapist's intentions. Although one can debate whether it is proper to hold such a goal for a client who is not a Christian (this is a matter to which we will return) it must be admitted that the furtherance of a *Christian* client's spiritual life is an *intrinsic* part of the healing process. While the brain surgeon or the civil engineer may be able to sort his or her professional activities and religious convictions into separate compartments, this is not so neatly done by the psychological helper. The personal convictions of the mental health professional are, like it or not, a strong influence on the kinds of interventions he or she is likely to make in people's lives.

The Christian church in this century faces a formidable challenge. Always the church has had benefactors and detractors, friends and enemies, but rarely have these so strikingly been one and the same. A single professional discipline (psychology) is currently among both the church's greatest resources and its fiercest rivals. The benefits that the church stands to receive from psychology are enormous. Yet unless Christians can come to proper terms with psychology, an increasing percentage of hurting and broken human beings are likely to leave the church. It is possible, of course, for one to leave spiritually but not physically, to retain one's place in a social institution long after abandoning its deeper values and beliefs. This is what a good many people, frustrated in their needs for healing, seem to be doing.

Psychotherapists and other clinical counselors have effectively cared for lots of persons who otherwise would have been neglected, inside as well as outside the church. Mental health practitioners have managed to find ways to help that are often glaringly and regrettably missing in the local congregation. Where the church has sometimes tended to apply only the cosmetics of platitudes, therapists have prescribed the powerful remedies of empathy and wisdom. In the process, however, many secular therapists have smuggled into the lives of their clients a great deal of anti-Christian gobbledygook. Christian therapists naturally regard this as tragic.

In the chapters that follow, I am going to try to clear away some of the confusion that has hindered our understanding of how theology and psychology fit together. What I will share with you is the result of a soul-searching intellectual struggle. The struggle has come from trying to peer into what at times seems like a dense jungle. This conceptual density comes from the fact that both disciplines (psychology and theology) help us discover the nature of human personality as well as how to change it for the better. Both lay claim to the human heart.

Christian theology describes the processes of conversion, regeneration, and sanctification. Contemporary psychology suggests such methods as verbal psychotherapy, crisis intervention, and behavior modification. As a Christian psychologist, I have tried to figure out something of how the concepts of the theologian and those of the psychologist intersect. Are what the theologian calls sin and what the psychologist calls psychopathology really the same thing? Are conversion, regeneration, and sanctification simply different labels for what happens to a person who consults an effective psychotherapist? Are theology and psychology, after all, just two parallel language or symbol systems—two paradigms for the same phenomena?

In dealing with such questions, there are two very easy ways to end the intellectual struggle to which I have referred. We have already mentioned one of them. It is to insist that psychology and theology have nothing to do with each other; that they are entirely independent. Theology has to do with matters of "faith," so the argument goes, while psychology concerns matters of "fact." Christian regeneration and psychotherapeutic growth have nothing in common, except perhaps that they both make people feel better and both are "good."

The second way out of the struggle is to collapse one

discipline into the other. Atheistic psychologists do this when they suggest that, since there is no God, all talk about God is merely an expression of the speaker's psychodynamics or reinforcement history. Certain Christians do much the same thing, only in reverse. They insist that psychology and psychotherapy are illegitimate. There is no such thing as a psychological problem that cannot be taken care of by repentance of personal sin and more intense piety. All psychological difficulties are, thus, evidence of inadequate faith.

As I will attempt to demonstrate, both of these ways out of the struggle are ill-informed. Each offers a solution that, however comforting in the moment, turns out ultimately to be misleading. Just as there is no final way out of the tension between Law and grace, there may be no escape from the conceptual and practical problems that arise out of the attempt to integrate psychology and theology. Total absorption in Law produces a poisonous legalism unmitigated by love, while reliance on what Dietrich Bonhoeffer called "cheap grace" yields license and anomie. There is always a dialectic between Law and grace. There is also a dialectic between theology and psychology that on this planet is unlikely to fade away for our convenience. Easy answers are, alas, not answers at all!

NOTES
1. R. F. Fortune, *Sorcerers of Dobu* (New York: E. P. Dutton & Co., 1963).
2. Jerome D. Frank, *Persuasion and Healing: A Comparative Study of Psychotherapy* (Baltimore: The Johns Hopkins University Press, 1961).

ONE
THE CRITICAL NEED
FOR INTEGRATIVE THINKING

Many Christians are convinced that psychotherapy
is valuable. Some of us have come to this conclusion
by watching a psychologist treat a troubled relative.
Others of us have come to it through personal
involvement in the therapeutic process. Regardless of
how individual Christians decide that psychological
services have value, they are likely to sense tension
between Christianity and psychotherapy.

Some Christians feel guilty about having been in
psychotherapy and yet, at the same time, well know that
it was very beneficial to them. They may rarely talk
about the subject, however, because they do not want to
incur the disapproval of others. Where secretiveness
rules, ignorance prevails.

The church has generally regarded psychology either
as an overt threat to religion or as just so much
nonsense. Rarely has sufficient attention been paid to
the distinction between what psychologists do and
what psychologists say about what they do.

There is an important difference between method and
ideology. Separating the two is not always easy, and,
as a result, psychology has acquired something of a bad
reputation in certain quarters. This has prompted many
Christians to reject psychology, even though certain
therapies have proven themselves very helpful to people.

Psychology As Selfism. The most troubling ideology at this point in history is what New York University professor Paul Vitz calls "selfism."[1] In his book, *Psychology As Religion*, Vitz describes how he took his Ph.D. at Stanford, how one day he realized that he was saying things in lectures that he did not believe, and how by the late sixties he had reached the place where he simply "would no longer teach graduate or undergraduate courses that required [him] to cover self-theorists." What especially delights me is Vitz's statement on page 12 that sometime after 1972 he "discovered [he] was a Christian."

In a review I wrote of the book, I said it was "likely to send shock waves through the intellectual community to which it was addressed."[2] It has. Karl Menninger, perhaps the foremost American psychiatrist at that time, called it the most satisfying book he read that year, adding, "It says what ought to have been said long ago —bravely, clearly, and constructively."

What Vitz had caught hold of was the total illegitimacy of panning off on the public as "science" a values system that puts "feeling good" at the center of everything. He argued, with considerable force, that such a values system clashes head-on with a number of Christian norms, for example, a concern for one's neighbor that parallels the concern for oneself.

Critiques of self-absorption have also come from secular sources. The year after Vitz published his book, Christopher Lasch, a historian from the University of Rochester, brought out his bestselling *Culture of Narcissism.*[3] Unlike Vitz's book, which ends on a note of Christian hope, Lasch's seems tinged with despair. Nonetheless, it shoots well-aimed arrows into the heart of those selfist values reflecting at least part of what he labels our "dying culture."

Regardless of whether or not the American way of life is in peril, Christians need to scrutinize and lovingly challenge the navel-gazing egocentrism that permeates it, *especially* when this egocentrism is promulgated by psychologists in the name of science. However, to issue *responsible* challenge requires understanding.

Psychology's Attack on Religion. We should note in passing that Christians have become skeptical of the psychological professions for more reasons than the rise of selfism and the narcissistic turn of mind. There is also the overt attack on religion that has been coming from members of these professions for over fifty years. Consider Freud's *Future of an Illusion,* or his *Moses and Monotheism.*[4] These pieces were written, respectively, in 1927 and 1939. More recently, Harvard psychologist B. F. Skinner kindled the ire of religiously sympathetic people with his 1971 book, *Beyond Freedom and Dignity.*[5]

Psychology, Theology, and Religious Values. Neither psychology nor theology can do the other's job. The truth of this statement may not be self-evident, so I would like to present some of my reasons for making it.

Psychology is simply not theology, nor should it try to be. Many of its researchers and practitioners have abandoned traditional religion. They might respond more openly to an astrology lecture than to a reasoned presentation of the Christian gospel. This remains true, despite the fact that there has always been a minority of psychologists interested in the study of religious behavior. Some behavioral scientists, while quick to inject metaphysical or ethical affirmations into their work, are just as quick to complain if the thing injected is Judaism or Christianity. They point out that matters of religion do not belong in the domain of science. In this they are right.

The issue is whether any comprehensive psychology can be all that scientifically pure, particularly if it is to be used in the clinic with real, live, hurting people. Furthermore, if we concede the impossibility of such purity and acknowledge with Perry London[6] and others that psychotherapists function partly as secular priests, on what justifiable basis can psychologists reject the intellectual infrastructure of the Western world, while blithely welcoming all kinds of spiritual esoterica? The issue of where open-mindedness stops and superstitious foolishness begins is moot.

Psychology, as we have it today, is the offspring of a

nineteenth century union between philosophy and physiology, with minor contributions from enterprises as diverse as astronomy and hypnotism. Psychology began as an attempt to answer old questions with new techniques, specifically the techniques of the physical sciences. Gustav Fechner, for example, one of the earliest psychologists and the father of experimental psycho-physics (how sensations are related to stimuli), set out to measure the effects of physical stimulation on the soul. His 1860 *Elements of Psychophysics*, a landmark volume in behavioral science, was the tangible expression of these efforts.

But such religious interest on the part of psychology's leaders did not last long, except in rare persons like Harvard professors Gordon Allport and William James.[7] Certain psychologists, of course, did continue to investigate religiously oriented questions (there is a division of the American Psychological Association for psychologists interested in religious issues), but they never became much of a dominant influence on the profession. The emergence of psychology as an independent discipline signified the rise of a radical humanism that was to show religion little sympathy.

It is sometimes suggested that psychology came into being partly because of two humiliations to the human species—the Copernican theory (1543), which asserted that the earth was not the center of the universe but that the planets revolved around the sun, and the work of Charles Darwin (1859), who advanced the theory that man had evolved from lower forms of life. I would like to argue, however, that the emergence of psychology represented an unprecedented preoccupation of people with themselves. This preoccupation was given considerable encouragement by the shift in modern thought that resulted from the writings of Descartes (1596-1650).

The exploration of "inner space" began to be extremely important, which was partly reflected in increased leisure and affluence as well as in the proliferation of academic specialties. Modernity's focus on psychological issues has been both boon and bane; boon in that it reflects appreciation for the worth and nobility (re: *imago Dei*) of humankind, and bane in that it seems to have accelerated the wholesale neglect of religious questions. A fair number of psychologists and psychiatrists, explicitly or implicitly, hold the view that religion is outdated if not, by nature, psychopathological.[8] Such blind prejudice has led to psychology's abandonment of a spiritual heritage that has something infinitely and eternally valuable to give men and women.

The Church's Need for Psychology. Systematic theologies focus on God and tend, rightly or wrongly, to neglect psychological processes. Some theologians seem purposely to ignore the experiential foundations of knowledge. The subjectivist twist given to theology by Schleiermacher and Feuerbach in the nineteenth century has understandably given many theologians pause before embracing anything with a psychological cast to it.

A "subjective point of departure" in no way imperils the objectivity of truth, as I will show in the next chapter. At the same time, religious epistemologies (theories of knowledge) that explicitly rest on experience have so often led to denials of objective truth that many theologians have grown wary of the psychological. This has led, in turn, to the neglect of psychological matters.

The "fruits of the Spirit" are by nature psychological, and they appear to have a lot to do with what it means to be fully human.[9] Happiness, joy, peace, etc., are experiential, subjective by definition. They are states of consciousness about which God seems vitally concerned, at least if we judge from the first Psalm or the fifth chapter of Paul's letter to the Galatians. Despite these things, except in very circumscribed ways, systematic theologies attend hardly at all to complex psychological phenomena.

Maybe this is as it should be. After all, theologians are theologians and psychologists are psychologists. Unfortunately, theologians have at times been among the most outspoken critics of psychology, tending grossly to oversimplify the nature of human psychological struggle and to underestimate the intricacies of our mental processes. If psychologists have psychologized theology, theologians have theologized psychology.

Turning to theology's outworkings in the church, Christians have not always been completely effective in dealing with emotional troubles. It is not all that hard to understand why. Christianity is *supposed* to change one's life. The question is whether the change is entirely the result of piety—of one's direct relationship with God—or whether it sometimes requires other people. I will contend that the critical role of other Christians, of the body of Christ, has been glossed over.

This glossing over of the *ecclesiological* dimensions of emotional healing has come from a combination of conceptual fuzziness and ill-informed perfectionism. The conceptual fuzziness, which has to do with the nature and mission of the church, is at root the proper concern of the theologian. As a psychologist, however, I would like to say something about perfectionism.

Christians seem to live with two beliefs that cause us no end of grief. On one hand, everyone knows that he or she suffers at least a little from anxieties, conflicts, irritabilities, moodiness, and a number of other routine human frailties. On the other hand, Christians have tended to imply, and often to proclaim, that these sorts of ubiquitous troubles are due to unconfessed sin, insufficient faith, and so on. The knowledge we have of our own imperfections, coupled with the guilt we feel in response to them, creates at times a thick atmosphere of guardedness. We are afraid, sometimes with good reason, that others will castigate us for our frailties. If we could only accept that we have failed, that we fail daily, and that we will continue to fail in the future!

We seem inveterately committed to social hierarchy, even within the church, where we often grade people on their moral appearances. The doctrinal assertion that we are *all* imperfect sinners has not deterred Christians from hiding their psychological hurts and struggles, out of fear that these imperfections would reveal moral failings and thus lead to social censure. The simple truth is that we are all fallen creatures and that, on earth, we will always be fallen creatures! Claims to psychological or moral perfection are just untrue.

We will return, in later chapters, to the question of what can and cannot be expected to happen psychologically when a person comes to faith through Christ. For now, let us note only that the doctrine of regeneration in the New Testament does not entail making us into gods, or into perfect copies of Jesus. Change is always measured relative to some very human starting point. As George Ladd[10] says of the Kingdom of God, salvation is both "already" and "not yet." Christian maturity is a path and not an achievement. The stubborn refusal of Christians to admit the plain truth about their own lives has been perhaps the greatest sin of all. It is, in fact, the sin of pride.

The Reaction against Psychology. The worst damage may be done, however, by persons who are *neither* psychologists nor theologians. What, to me at least, is a troubling example of questionable opinion are some of Jay Adams's writings.[11] These, for some reason, appeal to large numbers of Christians who sincerely want to help others. This appeal is probably due, in part, to the seductive simplicity of Adams's view that all nonorganic psychological problems are a direct result of sin and can be remedied by decisions to walk more closely with God.

Consider the title of his bestseller *Competent to Counsel*—as if reading one book, and, at that, a book written by someone who is not a mental health professional, could make a person into the complete human helper!

The appeal of Adams's work may also be attributable to the fact that such a view offers to ameliorate precisely those tensions that we are considering in this book. You simply get rid of psychology *qua* psychology. The number of people, if any, who have been dissuaded by such books from seeking competent *professional* help when it was needed is impossible to determine.

Adams's bold pronouncement that there is an intimate connection between the spiritual and the psychological contains more than a kernel of truth. Most Christians well know that their spiritual lives and their emotional states have *something* to do with each other. They realize that psychological problems and spiritual problems are somehow related, but the nature of this connection is very hard to explicate.

While I do not agree with Adams's position—it is simplistic—I can appreciate what might have motivated him to develop it. Sensing that psychology and psychiatry had, at times, tragically neglected and discounted legitimate religious questions and concerns, and that the church and its intellectual leaders had failed to minister to countless people in deep emotional pain, something had to be done. Adams did what he knew how to do. Unfortunately, he also tried to do what he did not know how to do.

What *is* the relationship between sin and neurosis? Between health and spirituality? Between deceit and defensiveness?

The mind-boggling difficulty of these questions —when they are honestly and maturely addressed— shows how hard it is to say anything intelligent about how theology and psychology interpenetrate.

The Reaction against Theology. A sense of this interpenetration is what may have led some psychologists to see in one or another form of psychotherapy the embodiment of living Christianity. Tired as most Christian psychologists are of overly cerebral religion, we find some of them reacting against "propositional theology." By "propositional" they usually mean "systematic" or "doctrinal." They seek "embodied integration."[12]

Stated this way, one can hardly take exception. It is easy to notice the way in which large sectors of Christendom seem to have reduced faith to a series of dry, verbal exercises. However, one cannot legitimately talk about a "propositional" versus a "nonpropositional" theology. To do this reflects either muddled thinking or the worst kind of anti-intellectualism. All theologies are, by nature, systems of doctrinal propositions. What matters are the specific propositions to which one adheres.

Ideas may not be the whole ballgame—surely they are not. But without ideas there is *no* ballgame! Cognitions (thoughts) may be insufficient by themselves, but they are inescapable. The issue is not theology versus no theology. In the domain of theological-psychological integration, the latter is an impossibility. As James Daane insightfully comments in his response to lectures given by Walter Houston Clark, "a psychology without theology develops a theology of its own."[13]

To give just one example of the problem to which Daane is alluding, we hear much talk these days about "relational theology." Such a theology may or may not be compatible with historic Christianity, depending on what one means by "relational."

I have heard this word used to emphasize the centrality of *interpersonally* living out the fruits of the Spirit. My own church, First Presbyterian Church of Hollywood, puts a lot of time and energy into this kind of caring. For this I am grateful. It is a great blessing to be part of a community of believers to whom the needs of other people matter.

Instead of supplanting Christian *kerygma* (proclamation of the gospel), good relational theology simply carries *kerygma* to its logical conclusion. It says, in essence, that human relatedness is of pivotal importance in Christianity. Caring for human beings and treating them with loving concern is at the center of a dynamic faith in the living God.

Regrettably, some relational theologies are based on assertions that are contrary to historic Christianity. One version suggests that the perfecting of human relationships is intrinsically evangelistic, whether or not the therapist *ever* acknowledges the universality of sin, humankind's need for redemption, and Christ's saving work. Calvin Schoonhoven, however, in a response to lectures by Thomas Oden, forcefully asserts that "conceptualization is an indispensable factor in the faith process."[14] Can one be said to know Christ if one has no viable conception of who Christ is?

Secularizations of Christianity only damage our understanding of it. While we must admit that these have often been formulated in reaction—usually in reaction to an accurately perceived human need—often they have nearly destroyed the theology they were designed to rehabilitate. Responding to an ailing viscera, as it were, the secularizers have pulled it out of the body, hooked it up to artificial life support systems, and then mistaken the grotesque result for a complete and healthy organism.

The Challenge. We need a set of understandings that will articulate the connections between theology and psychology, without reducing one to the other or trivializing either's rightful concerns. Just as there is no ultimately definitive systematic theology but, rather, many profitable theologies of the Christian faith, there is and probably never will be a "final" psychological-theological integration. Perhaps the most we can hope for is the resolution of some troublesome questions.

Such a resolution would be no small accomplishment. It would probably lead to a genuine easing of tensions in the border territories between the two disciplines. It might also encourage Christians to draw more readily, and with less guilt, from the assets of the various approaches to psychotherapy.

There is absolutely nothing in behavioral science that refutes Christian belief, as good integrative thought will show. If the church were truly convinced of this, a good many more of its members might avail themselves of the valuable tools and findings of psychology.

Recall Galileo and how much trouble he got into when he discovered the moons of Jupiter. Everyone *knew* that there were only seven heavenly bodies, seven being an immutably sacred number. Churchmen of his day refused to look through his telescope. They said it generated "illusions of Satan."

Some Christians are still afraid to look through the telescope, at least when it is trained on psychological phenomena. They need reassurance. To people who think they have found in behavioral science a refutation of the Christian faith, we must issue the invitation to look once again.

Christians in the latter part of the twentieth century must somehow navigate between two potential sources of disaster: the Scylla of neglecting to use the rich healing resources of psychology, and the Charybdis of constructing, from the misguided thought-forms of certain psychologists, the only new heresy to come along in hundreds of years—psychology as salvation.

The best charts for navigation will probably develop out of extended discussions between theologians and psychologists. Without such discussions, each discipline will likely go its own merry way, while the *people* both should be serving either continue to suffer unnecessary psychological pain, abandon Christianity, or both.

NOTES
1. Paul C. Vitz, *Psychology As Religion: The Cult of Self-Worship* (Grand Rapids: Eerdmans, 1977). For an insightful commentary on the heritage of modern self-absorption, see Peter Marin, "The New Narcissism," *Harper's* (October 1975), pp. 45-56. Also see Shirley Sugerman, *Sin and Madness: Studies in Narcissism* (Philadelphia: Westminster, 1977).
2. *The Journal of Pastoral Care* 23 (1978):139.
3. Christopher Lasch, *The Culture of Narcissism: American Life in an Age of Diminishing Expectations* (New York: Norton, 1978).
4. *The Standard Edition of the Complete Psychological Works of Sigmund Freud* (London: Hogarth Press), 21:3-58, 23:3-140.
5. B. F. Skinner, *Beyond Freedom and Dignity* (New York: Alfred A. Knopf, 1971).
6. Perry London, *The Modes and Morals of Psychotherapy* (New York: Holt, Rinehart and Winston, 1964).
7. William James, *The Varieties of Religious Experience: A Study in Human Nature* (New York: Macmillan, 1905/1961).
8. Claude Ragen, H. Newton Malony and Benjamin Beit-Hallahmi, "Psychologists and Religion: Professional Factors and Personal Belief," *Review of Religious Research* 21 (spring 1980):208-217.

9. See José Ortega y Gasset, *What Is Philosophy?* (New York: Norton, 1960).
10. George Eldon Ladd, *A Theology of the New Testament* (Grand Rapids: Eerdmans, 1974).
11. Jay Adams, *Competent to Counsel* (Grand Rapids: Baker, 1970).
12. For example, see Kirk Farnsworth, "Embodied Integration," *Journal of Psychology and Theology* 2 (spring 1974):116-124.
13. James Daane, "Psychologized Religion: Its Egocentric Predicament," in Walter Houston Clark, et al., *Religious Experience: Its Nature and Function in the Human Psyche* (Springfield, Ill.: Charles C. Thomas, 1973), p. 74.
14. Calvin R. Schoonhoven, "The Theological Substructure of Oden's Theology and Psychology Synthesis," in Thomas C. Oden, et al., *After Therapy What?: Lay Therapeutic Resources in Religious Perspective* (Springfield, Ill.: Charles C. Thomas, 1974), pp. 115-135, particularly pp. 125-129.

TWO
KNOWLEDGE, FAITH, AND SCIENCE

Philosophy is the academic discipline that has most to
do with ideas for their own sake, rather than with ideas
in the service of something else. Before we continue our
discussion, I would like to bring into view some
elementary but important material from epistemology,
that branch of philosophy having to do with how people
know things.

Our particular concerns deal with the kinds of things
that can be discovered, or verified, through scientific
psychology. Mental health professionals, as well as
laypersons, are often confused about exactly what sorts
of questions science can and cannot answer.

As a result, it is common for people to look toward
scientists for philosophical and religious guidance, as if
laboratory expertise somehow ensured wisdom. To
make matters worse, the practice of psychotherapy is an
amorphous mixture of applied science and clinical
philosophy. Some of this clinical philosophy is informed
and sophisticated, but much of it is amateurish.
Knowing which is which is not always easy.

The Nature of Basic Assumptions. The single most
important idea we can draw from the philosophy of
knowledge is that primary (major) premises are not

demonstrable. This is a fancy way of saying that you cannot "prove" the truthfulness of basic, rock-bottom beliefs. To prove anything means to demonstrate that it necessarily follows from something else. If this *something* that you are trying to prove follows from something else, then the "something else" is really primary and the *something* secondary.

Stated differently, if you could prove the "truth value" of your basic beliefs, it would be because you appealed to other beliefs—but then you would face the problem of proving *those* beliefs. Eventually, if you push the demand for proof far enough, you arrive at something that has to stand on its own, some idea or set of beliefs that you take to be ultimate and, therefore, not in need of proof. This something is, to you, self-evident.

How anyone reaches what, to him or her, is self-evident is a difficult question. This question is the principal concern of philosophical and psychological epistemologists and is beyond the scope of our discussion. Let us simply note that a person's fundamental beliefs develop in subtle ways that involve much more than straightforward logic.

I want to illustrate what I am talking about with two imaginary dialogues:

Person A: "Do you believe in God?"
Person B: "Yes, of course."
A: "Why?"
B: "Because the Bible says there's a God."
A: "But how do you know the Bible is true?"
B: "Because God wrote it."

The hopeless circularity in this dialogue is obvious. Let us assume that the interchange goes a little differently:

A: "How do you know that God exists?"
B: "Because the universe is so beautiful. There must be a God who created it."
A: "I don't think so. It's all just chance."
B: "But look, there has to be a creator!"
A: "Why?"

B: "*Because the universe is so beautiful . . . .*"
A: "*Okay, let's skip that for the moment. How do you know the universe is, as you put it, beautiful? To me it's ugly.*"
B: "*Just look at it! Look at the mountains, the forests, the oceans. Look at the sunset and the night sky.*"
A: "*I will, if you look at all the little children dying of cancer; or the thousands of people who die every day of malnutrition.*"

The important existential questions—questions about God and the ultimate meaning of life—are not fully answerable through logical argument. "All men are mortal. Socrates is a man. Therefore, Socrates is mortal." That works fine on the chalkboard, but it does not always seem to have much to do with everyday life.

Attempts by some Christian apologists to "prove" Christianity have left many people frustrated. Such people read the apologists' books, try to use the rationalistic ideas and methods contained in them for "winning souls," and, more often than not, either fall on their faces or become unconscionably rigid and argumentative. In moments of evangelistic passion, they try to convince others through "reason" that God exists, that Jesus was resurrected, and so on. Then they get angry or depressed when their efforts fail. "I must not have fully understood what it said in so-and-so's book," I imagine them muttering. What, in fact, they have not understood is something the famous mathematician Blaise Pascal said centuries ago—the heart has its reasons which reason knows nothing of.

Arguments for the existence of God are not new. They have taken a number of classic forms, such as the "ontological argument" and the "argument from design."[1] Although these arguments have been around for a long time, the most they can accomplish, by themselves, is to bolster *existing* belief. They simply do not compel people to love God. If they did, the world would already be Christian.

Reasoned discourse may help to bring many people to faith, but it is not sufficient by itself. Something else is needed. If reason alone *were* sufficient, a person's intelligence quotient (a pretty fair estimate of reasoning ability) would enable us to predict whether or not he or she would make a faith commitment. Christianity would be a religion of the intellectual elite. But this, of course, is not so. We all know some brilliant people who are atheists (or at least some brilliant people who *claim* to be atheists, since it is an open question whether *any* human being can honestly maintain the nonexistence of God).

(One can argue, of course, that recognizing Jesus Christ for who he is demonstrates the only kind of intelligence that ultimately matters. Such an assertion radically alters what we ordinarily think of as intelligence. Instead of designating the capacity to think, intelligence becomes the willingness to endorse a given belief system:

A: *Why should I believe what you tell me about Christ?*
B: *Because it is true, and intelligent people know it.*
A: *What does it mean to be intelligent?*
B: *To believe what I do about Jesus Christ.*

This gets us nowhere.)

It is true that many people might never have become Christians without at least one other person taking the time and trouble to meet their intellectual questions with honest and well-thought-out answers. This does not imply, however, that mere intellectual dialogue can lead anyone to faith. Something beyond logic—God's Holy Spirit—must change the basic premises on which we build our lives.

Now I am not lobbying for irrationalism or subjectivism. Christianity *does* make sense, and there *is* a God. To say that beliefs are reached, in part, through nonrational processes is *not* to say that they are illogical or that they do not reflect a reality beyond themselves. At issue is how far logical reasoning can take us. When it comes to religious beliefs, it may not take us very far at all.

These comments, with minor modification, apply to any metaphysical or ethical belief. Although just about any statement can be used to begin a logical proof, basic metaphysical or ethical assertions cannot themselves be logically derived.[2] A great deal, therefore, rests on what assertions one makes primary, on what beliefs and values one takes as the foundation for everything else.

Scientific, Philosophic, and Theological Questions. Basic religious questions have very little, if anything, to do with science. The distinction between a philosophic and a scientific question is well drawn in this passage from Bertrand Russell's *History of Western Philosophy:*

Almost all the questions of most interest to speculative minds are such as science cannot answer. . . . Is the world divided into mind and matter, and if so, what is mind and what is matter: Is mind subject to matter, or is it possessed of independent powers? Has the universe any unity or purpose? Is it evolving toward some goal? Are there really laws of nature or do we believe in them only because of our innate love of order? Is man what he seems to the astronomer; a tiny lump of impure carbon and water impotently crawling on a small and unimportant planet? Or is he what he appears to Hamlet? Is he perhaps both at once? Is there a way of living that is noble and another that is base, or are all ways of living merely futile? If there is a way of living that is noble, in what does it consist, and how shall we achieve it? Must the good be eternal in order to deserve to be valued, or is it worth seeking even if the universe is inexorably moving towards death? Is there such a thing as wisdom, or is what seems such merely the ultimate refinement of folly? To such questions no answer can be found in the laboratory.[3]

Our consideration of the nature of primary premises, and of the distinction between philosophical and scientific questions, is directly relevant to the

relationship between Christianity and psychotherapy.
While it is patently clear that Christian beliefs are not
scientific (using the word in its modern sense), it is less
obvious that much of what psychotherapists believe,
and do, is equally nonscientific. This will become
increasingly clear as we move, chapter by chapter,
through our discussion. For now, we shall simply note
that in trying to integrate concepts from Christianity
and psychology, it may be impossible to treat the ideas
from both domains as if they stood on an equal footing,
since this can leave us at times with two contradictory
religions. Christianity *is* the Christian's religion,
obviously, and religious beliefs (as we noted above) are
not mere "matters of science." When the ideas from
the two domains seem to conflict, it may be necessary to
choose between them.

Theory and practice in psychotherapy are especially
open to the intrusion of unverifiable belief systems
which often masquerade as scientific truth. This
happens because therapists are at least partially
"scientific," and because, as we noted above, many
people mistakenly believe that to be scientifically
informed is to be philosophically informed. This
happens also because hurting human beings do not
conveniently leave their existential questions in the
waiting room as they walk through the door of the
counseling chamber. Patients prevail on their doctors
for answers in areas where doctors often know no more
than their patients. Sometimes they know less. Moreover,
there seems to be a strong tendency in people to
expound their views of the world. The temptation for
professionals to do this occasionally outweighs
responsible modesty.

Philosophical statements by religious or nonreligious
therapists have absolutely no validity stemming from
science. A psychiatrist, psychologist, psychiatric social
worker, or marriage counselor has no special
qualification for dispensing opinions about the meaning
of life, the nature of the universe, or what is ethically
good. To cite an example, a therapist may correctly

advise a patient that he will feel better if he puts his ailing mother in a nursing home, but the therapist has no particular expertise on the question of whether it is morally right to do so.

The difference between psychological science on the one hand and psychological philosophy on the other is that the former, the science of psychology, can be shown to be true (through experiments, questionnaires, tests) while the latter, the philosophical aspects of psychology, cannot be demonstrated in the same way. Yet the public, especially counselees, may accept both as having the same weight of authority.

As I hinted earlier, the description of psychology as totally scientific is a romanticized portrayal, since even tough-minded psychologists find it nearly impossible to refrain from speculating about ultimate causes or from talking about metaphysics and ethics. Psychologists, especially therapists, quickly move from the region of *scientific psychology* to that of *philosophical psychology*. For certain applied problems, psychology is quite capable of remaining scientific. The question of whether aggressive behavior is potentiated by viewing television violence is such a problem. As stated, this is a straight-forward empirical question, even in light of the trouble we might have in coming up with good definitions of aggression. But most psychologists are not happy to stop at this point. They want to say something more, something about the nature of the person, which brings us right to the edge of the philosophical waters. It also brings us back, at least implicitly, to basic beliefs!

Christian theology is rigorous reasoning, grounded in revelation, about God and his relationships with people and the universe. These reasonings begin with Scripture, which is partly what distinguishes theology from philosophy. By virtue of beginning with a circumscribed base of authority, theology is only quasi-speculative, whereas philosophy is fully speculative.

Yet, while God is revealed more directly and clearly through the pages of the Bible than he is, say, through the pages of *Hamlet*, people sometimes come to vastly different conclusions about what God may be saying through Scripture. Most points of doctrine just cannot be verified as easily as a scientific principle, such as the law of gravity.

We are thus tossed onto the shifting sands of what we may call "existential epistemology" to distinguish it from abstract academics. It is one thing to ask, from the philosophical armchair, how people "know." It is quite another thing to ask this same question about a particular person, caught in a particular crisis, seeking help, in a particular therapist's office, with problems that have theological overtones.

Untangling the Gordian Knot. I want to illustrate how hard it may be to produce good integrative thought by briefly examining two integrative attempts. In one case, Christian thought was "integrated" with philosophy, and in the other case with paleontology.

Paul Tillich, perhaps more than any other theologian of the twentieth century, negotiated a career commonly regarded as, and explicitly intended to be, integrative. "As a theologian I tried to remain a philosopher, and conversely so," wrote Tillich.[4] Tillich claims to have spent his life trying to fit together Christian theology and secular philosophy—or, in his words, trying to bring the particular *logos* (word) of Christianity into line with the universal *logos.* His "method of correlation," according to which answers from Christian theology are fitted to philosophic questions, is what he termed an "answering theology."

As I think through Tillich's work, it seems integrative primarily in the sense that the language of one discipline (theology) is coordinated to the content of another (philosophy). Tillich seems continually to beg questions by the manner in which he poses them, insofar as the categories of secular philosophy enjoy a distinct advantage in his writings. It is always theology that has to do the answering, as if Christianity is forever being summoned to court. Clinging to a circumscribed set of philosophic concepts, yet retaining the idioms of

ns, in places, like the capitulation of classical
y to wishful thinking (Teilhard) or to
n (Tillich).

do any better? Can we integrate clinical
y and Christian theology without falling into
l quicksand?

des MacGregor, *Philosophical Issues in Religious Thought*
Houghton Mifflin, 1973), which is probably the finest
ts kind in existence. For a less authoritative but crisply
d overview of the standard theological proofs, see also
spers, *An Introduction to Philosophical Analysis*, second
lewood Cliffs, N. J.: Prentice-Hall, 1967), pp. 425-492.

des MacGregor, *Philosophical Issues in Religious Thought*,
24, especially p. 105. I am put in mind of Karl Barth's
nt on types of apologetics: "A bold apologetics proves to
ular generation the intellectual necessity of the theological
es taken from the Bible or from church dogma or from
more cautious apologetics proves at least their intellectual
ty." Karl Barth, *Protestant Theology in the Nineteenth*
Its Background and History (Valley Forge: Judson Press,
440.

d Russell, *A History of Western Philosophy: And Its*
ion with Political and Social Circumstances from the
Times to the Present Day (New York: Simon and Schuster,
p. xiii, xiv.

rpretation of History* (1936), p. 3. Cited in Kenneth
n, "Paul Tillich," in *Creative Minds in Contemporary*
y, ed. by Philip E. Hughes, second ed. (Grand Rapids:
ns, 1969), p. 449.

example, Paul Tillich, *Biblical Religion and the Search for*
Reality (Chicago: The University of Chicago Press, 1955).
wis critiques this view in a delightful essay entitled "The
of a Great Myth," in *Christian Reflections* (Grand Rapids:
ns, 1967), pp. 82-93. Creative or developmental
nism was not something for which Lewis had much
In another place he refers to it as a view with "all the
f religion and none of the cost."
n, *Creative Minds in Contemporary Theology*, p. 466.

Acworth, "Pierre Teilhard de Chardin," in *Creative Minds*
mporary Theology, pp. 407-442. Although Acworth on page
s make the distinction to which I refer in the text, on
he writes, " . . .it is clear that he [Teilhard] was so

eligion, Tillich may have unwittingly sacrificed the very
essence of the historic Christian faith. While Tillich's
writings are insightful in places, his overall integration
may not amount to very much.

Turning to our second example, Pierre Teilhard de
Chardin was a Jesuit priest. He was also a process-
oriented paleontologist who was much taken with a
kind of Bergsonian evolutionism. He stands rather like
the Alfred North Whitehead of Catholicism.

To understand Teilhard's thought, it is necessary to
have in mind the difference between evolutionary
progressivism, a metaphysical doctrine, and Darwin's
thesis of natural selection. The latter is simply a
hypothesis regarding the mechanism by which so many
species of plants and animals came to exist: animals
that survive enjoy the privilege of reproducing and, thus,
of passing on their characteristics to progeny.

This is what Spencer's phrase "survival of the fittest"
means. The fit prevail, mate, and genetically bequeath to
future generations whatever it was that allowed them to
prevail in the first place.

Note that, according to the Darwinian idea, giraffes do
not have long necks because they had to stretch to reach
for food (the inheritance of acquired characteristics is
the central thesis of Lamarckian evolution, not
Darwinian). According to Darwin and most American
biologists, some giraffes long ago had longer necks than
others—a genetic accident—and, because they did,
these giraffes survived while the others did not. Since
they could reach the food, which was both scarce and
highly situated in trees, they lived on and bred.

There is nothing teleological to this—no purpose, no
ultimate goal toward which everything is moving, no
intentionality. Neither is there reason to assume that
goodness, as opposed to badness, facilitates survival and
reproduction. Looking over the panorama of history, one
could well argue that brutality would have been an
advantage.

Some philosophers, notably Henri Bergson and
Teilhard, add to Darwin's thesis the supremely

optimistic belief that creation is evolving ever upward, toward greater expressions of excellence.[6] Our principal interest in Teilhard, as in Tillich, concerns his particular way of integrating Christian theology with secular thought.

Returning to Tillich, Hamilton highlights the trouble Tillich seems to have run into:

The attempt to serve two masters, respecting each equally, is obviously a perilous one. There is a large likelihood that theology will be lost in philosophy or vice versa. Tillich's claim is that there is a "basic identity" of the two, as well as a "qualitative difference." However, we must ask how Tillich knows that this is so.[7]

Hamilton is questioning *Tillich's* epistemology, specifically the sources of his basic ideas. A few sentences later Hamilton goes at the same problem from another direction:

Instead of presenting himself as a philosopher of religion, Tillich now comes forward as a philosophical theologian employing the method of correlation. In the method philosophy poses questions which theology answers. The difficulty which arises in connection with the method is that the answers seem to be dictated by the questions.[8]

This is an old problem. By virtue of how they are framed, questions tend to predetermine the nature of their answers.

To use a well-worn example, if someone asks you why you still beat up your spouse, you are immediately ensnared in a web of assumptions—that you have a spouse, that you are strong enough to overpower your spouse, and that you have done so in the past. Another example is the vacuum cleaner salesman who asks, "Do you want to buy the regular or the deluxe model?" Did you say you wanted to buy a vacuum cleaner?

When Tillich says that the particular *logos* of Christianity must be brought into relation with the

---

universal *logos*, he presuppo the latter, an assumption we this additional passage from

It would seem, then, that the "correlates" theological term much as the method of conso men with the armed forces.[9]

Teilhard is vulnerable to a fascinating chapter which, u distinguish always between Darwinianism,[10] Acworth po nature of Teilhard's basic the

One cannot help being struck the vigor, not to say arroganc truth of the theory of evolutio cannot help observing, at the advances no solid proof of th that, in fact, many of his argu such a proof cannot be given.

It may be worthwhile to ca encyclopedia—or a philosop discarded simply because it Whether the problem is more and Teilhard is an open ques to note how difficult it may b integrative thought.

High quality integration—c call it, psychotheology—may courage.[13] Tillich wrote a boo Whatever he meant by this do involved straining to treat Chi philosophy as equals. Similar Teilhard. If Tillich and Teilhar maintain equality between the trying to integrate, they might challenging dilemmas instead

---

what seen Christiani secularism

Can we psycholog conceptu

NOTES
1. See Ged (Boston book of presente John H ed. (Eng
2. See Ged pp. 97-1 commer a partic principl both; a possibil *Century* 1959), p
3. Bertran *Connec Earliest* 1945), p
4. *The Int* Hamilto *Theolog* Eerdma
5. See, for *Ultimat*
6. C. S. Le Funeral Eerdma evolutio respect thrills
7. Hamilt
8. *Ibid.*
9. *Ibid.*
10. Richard *in Conte* 431 do page 4

completely under the influence of 'progressive' mythology, and of the theory of evolution *on which it is based,* that he sincerely believed he was translating the basic message of Christianity into modern times" (italics added).

11. *Ibid.,* p. 431.
12. E. Mark Stern and Bert G. Marino, *Psychotheology* (Paramus, N. J.: Newman Press, 1970).
13. Professor Ray S. Anderson, personal communication, June 12, 1976.
14. Paul Tillich, *The Courage to Be* (New Haven: Yale University Press, 1952).

THREE
PSYCHOTHERAPY
AND REGENERATION

Having pointed to the need for integrative thinking and having discussed some important ideas from the philosophy of knowledge, we will now take up how the changes resulting from psychotherapy compare and contrast with Christian regeneration—new life in Christ.

The Limits of Psychotherapy. I want to begin with a quotation that captures a pivotal truth. John Powell writes:

I do not mean to detract one iota from the contribution they make to the lives of wounded human beings, but clinical psychology and psychiatry must not be allowed to pose as saviors and redeemers. Therapy can never be a substitute for a life of faith. I knew, from my training in psychology, that no reputable therapists could ever promise this kind of "cure," this new "wholeness." There is no plastic surgery to remove the kind of psychological scars that all of us bear to some extent. By supportive psychotherapy we can be comforted, and by recon- structive psychotherapy we can be somewhat adjusted, develop new coping mechanisms, but . . . we cannot be healed or cured.[1]

Psychotherapy has its limitations. By itself, it will *never* do the radical work of restoring spiritual wholeness to the human person.

Psychotherapy is moving out of its infancy. It is coming to approximate a sophisticated art increasingly based on rigorous science. The program of any current psychological or psychiatric convention clearly conveys the impression that we are making progress.

As a clinical psychologist, I feel proud and hopeful. Psychology (and by implication, psychotherapy) is finally escaping its characterization as a "Wizard of Oz," who turned out in the end to be something of a fraud.

Psychotherapists are lifting depressions, alleviating anxieties, ameliorating fears, removing self-inflicted obstacles, managing more rewarding home environments, straightening out bizarre thoughts, providing needed reassurances, facilitating capacities for self-reliance, toning down over-reactions, inculcating proper sensitivities, increasing emotional freedoms, and in general teaching people a large number of personal and social skills. Quite an impressive showing!

Our concern in this chapter is whether psychotherapy by itself can ever get to the heart of the matter of human living, to regeneration in Christ, to what Christian theologians mean by the Greek word *metanoia.*

Reducing Faith to Treatment. Most Christian psychologists believe that there is *some* kind of positive connection between spiritual well-being and mental health. Yet, articulating the exact nature of this connection is very difficult, as I suggested in the first chapter.

All therapists know from experience that well-chosen words and actions in the consulting room can help people think, feel, and act better. All Christians know that faith in God, through Christ, tends to pull people toward goodness and peace. Since both psychotherapy and Christianity seem to lead to positive psychological change, the critical question becomes, what is the relationship between the two?

It proves an irresistible temptation for some therapists

to assert that the therapeutic process is equivalent to growing in faith. Many Christian psychologists set up what amounts to an identity between the two. They usually wind up saying something to the effect that sin is simply a theological term for neurosis. Ameliorating neurosis takes care of sin and automatically moves the person toward holiness.

Sin thus loses its distinctive ontological, or *lack* of ontological, status and is reduced to "nothing but" an intrapsychic or behavioral datum. It is no longer a terrible disruption of vertical and horizontal relationships, stemming from a fractured character structure vis-à-vis a fallen world, but rather a mere learned malfunction.

Such a view can be made to sound Christian by shifting the focus to human welfare and to the importance of human relationships. Still, from this perspective, both the *origin* of, and *remedy* for, sin are assumed to exist entirely on the human plane.

Surely one's defective relationship with God and with one's mother may express itself through exactly the same behaviors, e.g., irascibility, mistrust, and depression. If we limit our attention to overt and covert behaviors, sin and neurosis may well seem to be the same thing.

As soon as you start talking about the past or the future, however, or about essential natures, the equation of sin and neurosis breaks down. As I have pointed out, the trouble with equating the two is that it implies that human methods alone, without benefit of supernatural intervention, are capable of obliterating sin and of restoring one's broken relationship with God. To become a regenerated child of the Creator, presumably one need only submit to the ministrations of a competent therapist. A continuity (without qualitative distinction) is assumed to exist between psychological treatment and personal encounter with God. Just as sin becomes another name for neurosis, spiritual rebirth is chalked off as an old way of talking about modern therapeutic healing.

To the Christian, the key difficulty here is that it is

hard to see how a nonbelieving therapist, however
proficient, could routinely lead people into a kingdom
that he or she may not inhabit, especially when entrance
into this kingdom is said to depend on repentance of
sin and faith in God through Jesus Christ. The absence
of Christian theological content is what troubles the
Christian, who cannot see how a therapy carried on
without reference to Christ could automatically lead a
person *to* Christ!

A variation on this theme is to insist that sin is a
particular *kind* of neurosis but that only a Christian
therapist can effectively meet the challenge of alleviating
those neuroses that happen to be sin. Since the
Christian therapist has experienced grace, he or she is
presumably capable of communicating God's love to
others and, thus, of ameliorating the sin-neurosis nexus,
even if the gospel is never mentioned. The truth is that
any psychotherapy carried on without reference to
Christ can hardly be said to be Christian.

Therapy As an Aid to Faith. Now, let me introduce a
complication. Is it possible that some people are unable
to respond to the gospel because they simply cannot
believe that God loves them? Could a therapist, such as
I have described, be instrumental in enabling these
people to come to faith? Might it even be that such a
therapist (a nonbeliever) would be better at facilitating
readiness for Christ than many openly evangelical
therapists? I believe the answer to all three questions is
yes. Certain persons seem unable to love God because of
psychological impairment (although, in some instances,
they may have the impairment because they refuse to
love God).

Consider a psychotic individual—there are millions
in our country alone. Many psychotic people seem
incapable of faith because their mental processes are
so jumbled. A certain class of medicines (pheno-
thiazines) are often effective in reducing psychotic
thinking. It therefore seems possible, with the help of a
pill, to so transform the consciousness of some human

beings as to enable them to grasp the basic content of Christianity. A simple chemical intervention appears to create the *potential for metanoia.*

For a good many nonpsychotic people, verbal psychotherapy may have the same effect. It is possible, for example, that a person may be unable to respond to God as a loving heavenly father until he or she experiences a certain kind of emotional healing having to do with his or her *human* father.

What became of psychotic people before the 1950s, when the first phenothiazine drugs were introduced? What of persons today who are so intellectually limited that they cannot understand anything that is said to them? What happens to them religiously?

I do not know the answers to these questions, but I think we ought to give God the benefit of the doubt, as it were, since it is foolishly arrogant to conclude that God is unconcerned about, or capricious toward, creatures he brought into being. His grace, we believe, can overcome any obstacle.

The crucial point to note is that *preparatory* human developments, such as growth through therapy, are not *in themselves* conversion or regeneration.

God in his benevolence employs mysterious means to work with all of us. Emotional release or facilitation, even in the office of an atheistic therapist, may well be God's way of helping a particular person. Behavior therapy (see chapter 9) might be part of God's intentions for someone else.

Nonetheless, it is important not to confuse the prelude with the symphony, the preface with the story. As a better metaphor, teaching someone to read is prerequisite to his or her reading Shakespearean plays. Learning to read may be comparable to what goes on in good psychotherapy. The institution of a capacity, however, does not guarantee its utilization. A person who has learned to read may spend every minute looking through comic books. A person healed of hurts in psychotherapy may turn even further from God, in pursuit of "the good life."

Mental Health and Christianity. The most psychologically intact person in the world, using "intact" in its conventional sense, may be a nonbeliever. We *can* insist that faith is a necessary part of mental health, as long as we recognize how we are using words.[2]

Mental health is not ordinarily taken to hinge on faith. As I outlined in an earlier book on clinical psychology for clergypersons, we customarily have in mind such predicates of health as satisfactory interpersonal relating, appropriate social behavior, awareness and responsibility, realistic judgment, emotional balance, task effectiveness, and communicational directness.[3] On these dimensions, I see no evidence to suggest that Christians are, on the whole, any better off than non-Christians.

Were we to locate a person of exemplary psychological well-being (again, in the customary sense of this term), who was nevertheless without faith, I would expect to see an aware and resilient person who could focus his or her energies well, especially in conversation, and who would be substantially free of mental conflict.

Here this person might part company with the Christian, who will rarely be conflict free (see Romans 6-8). Christians, we are told in Scripture, have two natures. They are caught up in cosmic war, in the struggle between good and evil. Far from hoisting the flag of Christian psychological superiority, I wonder if Christians might not be generally *worse* off than unbelievers, precisely because we live in a fallen world and are not always willing to draw on God's power to help us with the conflicts that result from trying to walk with him.

If Christians lived in the power of the Holy Spirit, they might do altogether better than non-Christians, but such living is rare. On the one hand, a Christian who yields his or her life to God, and who thereby enjoys the peace of Christ, certainly has a big start on transcending problems. On the other hand, someone who has experienced Christian rebirth but who does not walk in the Spirit may be in worse psychological straits than

before. Unhappily, this may be the rule rather than the
exception.

The Psychological Effects of Regeneration. What
psychological effects *can* be expected to result from
conversion and regeneration? By way of introducing this
question, consider the comment C. S. Lewis once made,
to the effect that a small act of kindness by a great
sinner may be worth more to God than a large one by a
prig.

Outward appearances, including what we may call the
objective merits of the act itself, do not reveal its true
moral value. In assessing the merits of someone else's
actions, one has to take into account the raw material
with which he or she accomplished them. Since this is
usually impossible to do with any certainty, we have
been cautioned in Scripture not to judge.

We can judge the *act* for its goodness or badness, its
moral beauty or ugliness, but we cannot get inside the
heart of the *actor* to see how he or she stands in relation
to the act. In a person with a poor digestion, says Lewis,
irritability may be nothing like the moral imperfection it
may appear.[4]

Another way of putting this, I think, is that one may
conceive of a human being as an organized collection of
habits and motivations. This is a static metaphor and, if
you want to get picky, you can insist that motivations,
too, are largely habitual. Still, this distinction will serve
us well in our discussion.

While habits, overt and covert behavioral patterns, are
usually acquired over the course of a lifetime and, as
such, are relatively fixed by adulthood, motives change
from day to day and minute to minute, even though in
a particular person they tend to proceed along thematic
lines. Through the agency of God's Spirit, a Christian
acquires a new set of motives, grounded at least partially
in a new way of perceiving the world and its relationship
to God.

Nevertheless, such new motives, however intense, are
not yet fixed. They have yet to become habitual and,

therefore, they have not altered the basic substrate, the bedrock organization, of personality. Only as an individual *grows* in Christ—as his or her new motives are allowed to channel behavior over a period of time, and as he or she gives the mind of God free reign—will the fundamental "stuff" of personality change. Such change is precisely what Christian growth entails and what the church, as a vehicle of teaching and social support, is designed to accomplish.

An Imaginary Example. Consider a person, whom we shall call Igor, of very foul instincts. He is insensitive, combative, and selfish, and we want to know how the Christian faith may affect him. Is it likely to rid him of his psychological problems? Will it provide him with the existential utopia promised by some evangelists? (Such evangelists remind me of a poster I once saw. It portrayed a disheveled drunk sitting at a bar. The caption read, "Booze is the answer . . . does anybody remember the question?" To some, religion is the answer to the unspecified question, whether it is how to put a man on Mars or how to raise your hamsters.)

Having come to faith, Igor may transcend his problems, so long as he lives in the Spirit. Let him relapse for a moment, however, and he will probably revert to his cantankerous self . . . at which point his neighbors, if they were ill-disposed to his new religious-ness in the first place, will no doubt say "I told you so!"

What they may fail to appreciate is that Igor, however terrible he may still appear, now has within him the Spirit of the living God. Igor *has* God and God has him. Regardless of how briefly, Igor has lived a transformed life, and he will probably do so again if others are not too discouraging and judgmental. Over the years, he may actually turn into a decent sort of chap.

What if Igor sees a psychotherapist? Assuming all goes well, together they will be able to alter the raw stuff of his personality enough so that, the next time he suffers a spiritual setback, he may be a little less offensive to his neighbors. In a manner of speaking, the therapy accelerates his acquiring the behaviors that are part of Christian maturity.

Psychological intervention, as it were, makes the job of the Spirit easier. It may also stretch Igor's behavioral and emotional capacities so that, while yielding to God's Spirit, he may feel and act better than he would have without the therapy.

No matter who the recipient is, Christian or otherwise, therapy will probably facilitate what Lewis calls "nearness of likeness," i.e., being close to God in the sense of resemblance.[5] Of itself, however, nearness of likeness doesn't necessarily mean "nearness of approach." The latter, says Lewis, comes when we are *least* like God, when we come to him in dependence, relying on grace, forgiveness, and mercy.

Only nearness of *approach* can bridge the gap between us and our Creator. Improving ourselves through psychotherapy will never, by itself, do it. As Lewis notes, proximities of likeness—say, becoming a healthier person via therapy—"in one instance may help, and in another may hinder, proximity of approach. Sometimes perhaps they have not very much to do with it either way."[6]

What, then, are we to make of psychotherapy and of psychotherapists? The latter make their living by relieving human misery and by augmenting nearnesses of likeness. Rather than constructing houses or fixing washing machines, they build persons. As a result, they may make it more likely for some people to come to God, through Christ.

Such people-building may lead to faith, but it does not guarantee it. Psychotherapy helps human beings become more what God intends them to be, but it does not, of itself, save them from their spiritual self-destruction. Psychotherapy usually functions within the sphere of what theologians call "common grace."

The question before the church is whether its members can overcome pride and pretense sufficiently to avail themselves of this grace! Can we admit that each of us is, in some sense, Igor?

The Goals of the Therapist and the Christian. The therapist wants to help people make the most out of their human potentials and so, whenever possible, to rid clients of personal handicaps such as unrealistic fears, self-defeating attitudes, oppressive mood states, perceptual distortions, and maladaptive behavior patterns. Therapeutic methods range all the way from the straightforward giving of advice to deep emotional catharsis. Treatments between these poles include free association, behavioral training, non-directive listening, and lots of others, many of which we will discuss in chapters 9 and 10.

The Christian wants to help others know and love God and, in the process, to facilitate holiness. The primary obstacle to such holiness is sin. While it is useful to make the traditional distinction between Sin and sins, between Sin as a corruption tendency and sin in its specific behavioral manifestations, turning from particular sins usually seems to require that the person do something, through Christ, about Sin.

On the basis of Scripture, including both the Gospels and Paul's letters, it is difficult to make much of a case for practicing specific sins in order to root out the sin dynamic. Yet there may be times when a person has to choose between two sins or, at least, between breaking one of two laws. As we shall see, the choice often seems to be between explicitly violating a commandment and allowing a kind of emotional suicide to occur.

The focus of the discussion to come is the question of whether the two sets of intentions, those of the therapist and those of the Christian, ever come into conflict. While it is usually true that no incompatibility will be found between what is psychologically helpful and what conforms to biblical Law, is this always so?

No reasonable person would object to a therapist ameliorating a fear of open spaces, teaching a client how to get along better with family members, or increasing the ability of someone to make good management decisions at work. But we must ask, are Christianity and psychotherapy always such good bedfellows? Are there times when to encourage a client to do what, on the human plane, seems most therapeutic is also to beckon him or her away from what is usually considered to be Christian discipleship? Is it perhaps a well-intentioned but naive assumption that psychological growth and spiritual formation invariably walk hand-in-hand?

In the next chapter we will consider some factual clinical material. We will ask the uneasy question of whether there are times when breaking the Judeo-Christian moral code is "therapeutic," and if the Christian psychotherapist is ever caught in the miserable dilemma of having to choose between facilitating health (as mental health professionals traditionally define it), and fostering holiness, when the latter is said to involve keeping of the biblical Law. Will the therapist's adherence to, and advocacy of, Christian morality always aid the temporal psychological welfare of the client?

We have already addressed the question of how behavior may be affected by regeneration in Christ. In the following chapter, we will ask about the psychological effects of breaking the biblical Law. Will behaving in accordance with this Law *always* move a person in the direction of mental health? Will violating it *ever* do so?

I am intentionally using the terms "psychological welfare" and "mental health" in their customary senses to designate such qualities as self-esteem and self-awareness, emotional freedom coupled with adequate impulse control, social poise, and good judgment. Before we bring this volume to a close, we will ask if such conceptions are too limited. Given who we are as *created* persons, can a definition of psychological well-being be fully adequate if it does not take into account how we relate, or fail to relate, to the Creator?

NOTES
1. John Powell, *He Touched Me: My Pilgrimage of Prayer* (Niles, Ill.: Argus Communications, 1974), pp. 46, 47.
2. See Donald F. Tweedie, Jr., *The Christian and the Couch* (Grand Rapids: Baker, 1963).

3. Clinton W. McLemore, *Clergyman's Psychological Handbook: Clinical Information for Pastoral Counseling* (Grand Rapids: Eerdmans, 1974), pp. 21, 22.
4. For an excellent and highly relevant chapter, see C. S. Lewis, "Morality and Psychoanalysis," *Mere Christianity* (New York: Macmillan, 1943), pp. 69-73.
5. C. S. Lewis, *The Four Loves* (New York: Harcourt, Brace & World, 1960), pp. 11-21.
6. *Ibid.*, p. 21.

FOUR
LAW AND HEALTH

We are now going to investigate the relationship
between emotional health and religious obedience. Are
there times when the promotion of human psychological welfare requires the violation of God's Law?

Is the Christian sometimes faced with having to
choose between two kinds of goods that are, in certain
concrete instances, mutually exclusive? Living within a
fallen world in which good and evil are fibrously inter-
woven, do we occasionally have to select the lesser of
two evils? What is the duty of the Christian psychotherapist to a client confronting such a decision?

I would like to make it emphatically clear, at the
outset, that as Christians we are called to obedience,
even when such obedience *seems* to run counter to our
immediate emotional well-being. The sixth chapter of
Romans, which is pivotal to the material in this chapter,
treats definitively the question of whether we should
deliberately sin. Indeed, God's power-in-grace is to
enable us to love, serve, and obey him even when, on
the human plane, this seems impossible.

The Not-Too-Unusual Case of Robert. Robert was tall,
good looking, and not at all interested in Christianity,
at least not when we began working together. He was

timid and riddled with self-doubts. I began treating him when he was nineteen.

Many clinicians would have described him, at that time, as obsessive and seclusive. He was frightened by intimacy, unable to freely express feelings, limited in his social skills, and given to a detailed but private fantasy life.

Robert was the only child of a dentist who genuinely loved him but who, himself, was interpersonally awkward, and therefore never able to serve as much of a model of social poise. Moreover, the boy had been traumatized. His biological mother was harsh and unstable, and he was raised by a stepmother who eventually left Robert's father for a local businessman.

The dentist married a third time. His new wife was many years younger than he and, while feisty and demanding, she was also bright and intuitive. In retrospect, I think she had a lot to do with paving the way for some of Robert's changes.

There were additional psychological dynamics, of course, and Robert had vivid memories of courtroom battles between his biological parents concerning his custody. He also remembered that his father had taken a trouncing, financial and otherwise, from his previous stepmother.

Robert's shyness and social hesitancy significantly hindered the development of his interpersonal relation-ships, especially his ability to befriend and retain the attentions of girls. Caught between nearly paralyzing fears and an intense wish for a girl friend, Robert was in a terrible bind. I spent many hours listening to his expressions of frustration, including numerous reports of sexual dreams and fantasies.

It would be impossible, in the space available here, to describe much of what we did in our psychotherapy sessions, which continued for over a year. I saw him individually, got him to consult a young female psychological assistant, and for several months had him in a therapy group.

During our sessions, I tried to convey understanding

and acceptance to him, and to facilitate his compre-
hension of his own dynamics. I also gave him a fair
amount of behavioral homework, designed to get him
gradually to take more social risks. It was working. He
was growing.

An Unexpected Happening. Then one spring day, shortly
before I was going to have to end our work because I
was moving to another city, my struggling client
announced with joy that, on the previous night, he had
had intercourse with a woman several times.

A few months earlier, Robert had taken a room near
his college and had met an older student. The latter was
estranged from his wife, whom he had left in their native
European country. A "man of the world" with many
female friends, this man was eager to pass his
accumulated knowledge along to Robert.

The older student apparently explained Robert's social
problems to a woman who, as it turned out, was a
patient and understanding human being. When she was
introduced to him, she took the time and trouble to
nurture Robert slowly past his reticence and into what
turned out, for him, to be a memorable evening.

The psychological effects on Robert were striking. He
reported greatly decreased fears of women—which is
not surprising, insofar as this sexual encounter
resembled a group of clinical procedures, known as
desensitization, that we will discuss in chapter 9. He
also reported an increased willingness to initiate phone
calls to eligible women and to ask them for dates. His
overall self-confidence, as well as his valuation of himself
as a man, skyrocketed. Other considerations aside, what
psychotherapy researchers refer to as the "outcome" of
his one-night "treatment" seemed strongly positive.

Robert's new frame of mind and his augmented social
eagerness were neither illusory nor temporary. The
episode seemed to accomplish more for him than
traditional psychotherapy would ever have done.

I had mixed feelings about Robert's sexual experience.
This is because it *appeared* to have done him so much

good. He was not bothered at all by guilt, at least not that I could see, and the validation that he received from the encouter is hard to discount. He felt loved, valued, accepted.

What probably allowed me to feel this way is the unshakable belief I hold that God cares about people as ends in themselves. He cares about our *feelings*, about what makes us happy and about what makes us hurt. He agonizes when we agonize. If, as my good friend Audrey Beslow suggests, fear itself is perhaps a kind of sin (see Romans 8:14-17), God may have been delighted to see Robert get past his fear and emerge as a more fulfilled person—although I doubt that God was overjoyed with the particular event that enabled Robert to grow. In the ideal, Robert would have become a Christian and perhaps have married a loving Christian woman, who could have given him his therapy in the privacy of their bedroom. But he expressed *no* interest in Christianity.

Robert knew what I believed but would have none of it, saying he "would look into religion" after he got over his "more pressing problems." He was a good human being, by ordinary standards, but he was not concerned in the slightest, as far as I could tell, with God.

Had I greatly stressed Christian norms of sexual conduct, he would surely have found me toxic. As it stands, I expect that he will gratefully remember my clinic, recall that I took Jesus Christ seriously, and perhaps become misty-eyed, now and again, when he reflects on our moments of closeness—moments that were qualitatively different from anything he had experienced before. These things, I hope, will help draw him to God. Ironically, when we terminated therapy he said, with tears running down his face, "I couldn't have done it without you." He was referring to his emergence from fear.

The Haunting Question and a Tentative Answer. The core issue is whether breaking the Law can ever yield good.

Can it, upon occasion, facilitate health? Are ultimate and temporal "goods" always the same?

We are told in Scripture that sin yields its temporary pleasures. Maybe it also yields its temporary psychological benefits. In those cases in which the choice is between chronic emotional misery and temporary lawbreaking, what *is* one to choose? Is keeping the Law an end in itself?

Christian theologians believe that the Law is not arbitrary but functional. They believe that observance of the Ten Commandments, for example, does promote human welfare. Doing what God wants *is* best for people. The Law is not something to be discarded like so many old rags. Jesus said that he came not to destroy the Law but to fulfill it.

The problem revolves around the complexity of human existence as it concerns the Law. All moral dilemmas cannot be resolved simply by looking up a relevant principle, since sometimes two or more applicable principles stand in conflict. Refusing to come to grips with this complexity is a kind of moral cowardice.

Because the psychotherapist assumes the burden of nurturing people who cannot conveniently suspend such dilemmas while they are in therapy—in fact, the dilemmas are often what prompt them to seek help—it is imperative that the therapist be both humble and courageous in the face of a disturbing "moral fog." Most of all, the therapist must not judge the moral worthiness of the client, whose inner workings always remain something of a mystery.

The Christian psychotherapist does sometimes have to choose between supporting what is good, in the sense that it will help the client emotionally, and what is good in the sense that it conforms to the Christian ideal. Given that people consult us in the hope of improving their behavioral and emotional functioning, the problem is especially acute when the client, like Robert, is not a Christian and, so, does not hold Christian values.

The classic example of a vicious moral dilemma is the German Christian hiding a Jew during World War II. If you were in this position, and the Gestapo arrived at your door asking questions, what would you tell them? Would you lie, thereby breaking the prohibition against false representation, or would you adhere to the letter of the Law, allow the Jew to be taken, and then claim that you did the right thing, and that your hands were clean because *you* did not pull the trigger or turn on the gas?

In this situation, either telling a lie is not sin, even though it involves breaking the Law, or God wants us to sin. One seems to have to subordinate one moral principle—truthfulness—to another—the preservation of innocent life. There is no other alternative, unless, of course, you are of the opinion that a Christian in such a predicament should always tell the truth. Theologians in considering these kinds of dilemmas sometimes speak of a "tragic moral choice."

Why did I not advise Robert to have an affair, or even arrange for one? One reason is that I could not predict with certainty what the outcome would be. He *could* have come away from the experience laden with guilt, or it could have raised instead of lowered his heterosexual anxieties.

The most important reason, however, is that I do not choose to encourage violations of the moral Law, even if such violations *are* likely to produce temporal psychological benefits. Moreover, moral decisions which affect the client should be made *by* the client.

Whether breaking the Law in certain instances can facilitate temporal health and, if so, whether a particular person should choose health over Law are open questions. The Christian therapist may have something legitimate to say about the first question, but the second one does *not* fall within his or her rightful domain of professional functioning. The practitioner should point out the probable advantages and disadvantages of each course of action and leave it at that.

When I have discussed these issues with Christians, I

have found that "conservatives" want to deny that sin can ever promote emotional healing, and "liberals" want to deny that breaking the Law is sin. But can we live with the tension? Can we face the awful reality that, because and only because we are fallen creatures in a fallen world, sinning does sometimes make people feel better?

Had it not been for Robert's sexual interlude, he might have gone the rest of his life without getting over his fears. He could have continued on indefinitely as a frustrated, sad, and lonely person who wanted human intimacy even more than physical gratification, but having neither. I suspect that if something powerful did not happen about when it did, his avoidance behaviors would have become almost irreversibly ingrained. He was at a critical juncture in his development.

Some years ago I related this story to a Christian who suggested that what Robert needed was not an affair but a meaningful heterosexual relationship. I agree that such a relationship would have been beneficial, but, as we've just seen, the odds of it developing even with my help were slim. He did manage to date now and then, usually as a fourth to an unfinished threesome, but it never worked out. Always the relationship ended because the girl found him awkward. Each time this happened, his confidence further declined.

Beyond this, I am not sure that what he experienced was not a "meaningful" relationship. You can always challenge the "positive results" of his actions by insisting that the evidence is not all in. This is true. We cannot know what the effects will be in ten or twenty years. I do not see how anyone could deny that the purely subjective effects were positive, however, quite aside from their possible spiritual implications. Nevertheless, feeling good should *never* be the ultimate value for a Christian (cf. Jesus in Gethsemane).

While it is often possible to think up some ideal solution to a problem such as Robert's, such solutions are not always available. Consider the despairing woman who has lived with a physically abusive, sexually uninterested, and alcoholic husband for twenty years. What if she stands at the brink of initiating a divorce, feeling that her choice is between this and suicide?

All the therapy in the world may not solve the existential problems she confronts. Christian Law says no divorce except for adultery. Concern for her life may run counter to this Law.

Not wanting to usurp anyone's moral choices, I refrain from making this decision for clients, but from within the safety of this book I want to say, in the abstract, what I believe. Although it is true that none of us knows the future, what makes for ultimate moral good may not always be the same thing as what produces immediate emotional fulfillment.

We have considered the cases of an inhibited young man, an abused wife, and a Christian hiding a Jew from the Nazis. Additional cases presenting similar moral dilemmas are not hard to imagine.

Should a husband who cheated on his wife years before tell her so, on her death bed, if she asks about his fidelity?

Should a hungry man in India steal food for his family?

Should a government witness twist the truth in giving court testimony against a Mafia killer, when failing to do so might result in a morally outrageous acquittal?

While it is easy, in the abstract, to assert that ends do not justify means, excessive concern with the moral purity of means, to the neglect of the ends these may produce, seems foolish, irresponsible, and inhumane.

All Christian therapists have treated people who decided *not* to break the Law, when in the throes of a conflict such as those we are considering. I recently heard about the treatment of a student, years ago, who had been arrested several times for lewd conduct, including soliciting and performing homosexual acts in public bathrooms. After two years of regular psycho-therapy, he was invited to have intercourse by a young female co-worker. Wanting to follow what he believed to be God's will, he declined the invitation. His refusal seems to have been genuine and not a rationalization for lingering fear. The therapist supported his decision. Now, some twenty years later, the man is married, has children, and is effectively serving the church.

The question we have addressed in this chapter, however, is whether breaking the Law can *ever* lead to growth. We have discussed cases in which lawbreaking appears beneficial, but as we noted, what is of temporal psychological value may not always be of eternal worth.

In the next chapter we will consider the role of the Holy Spirit in psychological growth. Are there instances in which God's Spirit, acting in a person's life, accomplishes much more than anything we could reasonably expect solely on the human plane?

FIVE
SKEPTICISM
AND THE HOLY SPIRIT

Skepticism has been with us from the beginning. The saga of Adam and Eve is a story of encroaching doubt, of a turning from trust to reservation and, finally, to vacillation and rebellion. In the Genesis narrative, Eve's certainty is eroded by the taunting question, "Is it true that God has forbidden you to eat from any tree in the garden?"[1]

Having thrown her off balance with this hyperbole, the serpent moves in with a direct challenge to the divine imperative not to eat from the forbidden tree. Thus, watering the seeds of mistrust, the creature launches humankind on its tragic odyssey of despair mingled with hope, and of functional atheism—living as if there were no God. One does not doubt God from the safety of a neutral zone. In truth, there may not be any neutral zone.[2]

The Value of Doubt. Bertrand Russell, whom I quoted in chapter 2, was until his death the preeminent twentieth-century master of the short critical essay. He wrote some troubling things, such as "Why I Am Not a Christian,"[3] but the bulk of Russell's popular material is crisp, helpful, and logical. This last quality will come as no surprise to readers who recognize him as a mathematical logician.

Decades ago, Russell published a collection of essays that I especially like.[4] The book's introductory piece is entitled "On the Value of Scepticism."[5] In this essay, Russell goes after a number of sacred cows, among them the spirit of competition. He argues, with some power I think, that intellectual progress partly hinges on our ability to develop what he terms a "rational scepticism," particularly toward customs and superstitions.

As an approach to learning, doubt is often beneficial. Its acquisition is part of what has traditionally been called a liberal arts education. The attainment of a healthy skepticism is, in fact, a good part of what we usually mean by education itself. An educated person "does not believe everything in print."

Beyond Doubt. If the atheist were right, if there were no God, it might be reasonable to extend this skepticism to everything. We could take it all the way to solipsism, the assertion that the only thing that exists is one's own mind—everything else is fantasy, a mere intellectual dream.

But Christians believe that the atheist is not correct. We hold that God, in Christ, crashes through the barriers of our doubt. Upon our emergence as Christians, we decide God to be beyond the bounds of skepticism.

This decision is not all that conscious—it is more of a reflexive and deep inner response, informed by reason, than any kind of planned stance, and it is deeply personal. Yet its effects seem unmistakable. Though one may thereafter doubt this or that doctrine, or even whether God still cares about one's life, doubt rarely if ever extends as far as denying the existence of a personal God. While some believers eventually renounce their beliefs, these are the exceptions. Most Christians follow the rule of faith. The serpent is very crafty, however, and skepticism in the twentieth century has assumed a new disguise.

Imagine that you are introduced to a man who tells you that he has seen and talked with Jesus Christ, and that God has instructed him to tell people about it.

Imagine, further, that he claims to enjoy all sorts of "spiritual blessings" and, indeed, to be perfect in God's sight, and full of love. He also insists that he is replete with wisdom and that he is privy to God's secret plan. How long do you suppose it would take him to end up in a psychiatric facility? It is a good thing that the people in first-century Ephesus had no psychiatrists and psychologists, since the Apostle Paul made all of these claims.

The hardest part of witnessing to Christian faith in this era, particularly if you are a psychologist, is the risk that people will think you deranged or stupid. It is all right to pay lip-service to spiritual realities. Most good American church people do that. If you start to sound as though you truly *believe* what you are saying, however, you might experience something of what Jesus went through with *his* contemporaries.[6] Skepticism these days often wraps itself in the mantles of intellectual respectability and concern for "mental health."

Twentieth-century people have for the most part retreated from belief in the supernatural powers of an invisible God to the specious safety of the natural and the material. So many times I find myself labeling, insulating, doing whatever I can to avoid *risking* my intellectual, emotional, and behavioral welfare on an intangible God. Singed by the acetylene flame of the problem of evil, Christian therapists sometimes hide within the cocoon of professionalism, a skepticism that promises to protect them from surprises. While this cocoon of skepticism seems to cut life down to manageable size, thus providing a sense of control and of freedom from anxiety, it also prevents some therapists from experiencing the supernatural.

This leads me to make a more radical comment. If there is no supernatural in Christianity, then there is no Christianity.

There are too many references in the New Testament to the power of the Holy Spirit as integral to Christian faith for us to separate out, rationalize away, or relegate to a prior age the work of the Spirit. Christianity without transcendent clout atrophies either to a sterile metaphysical system or to a moral code which by itself can be oppressive.

I am not recommending that Christians flutter about from pillar to post, looking for their next spiritual high. There has been too much of that, and as a result the Holy Spirit has been given bad reviews. Some so-called charisma seems like frenzied attempts to halt, through "magic," the almost ominous silence we sometimes confront as we incline our ears toward the heavens.

However, once again we should not throw the baby out with the bath water. There may be a lot of gibberish getting passed off as spirituality, but this does not in any way negate the reality of God working in and through people. Is it possible that God's Spirit can affect a person's state of mind? Does God still do miracles?

The Case of Grace. Some years ago I was asked to evaluate a woman in her late forties. She was referred by a minister who had been seeing her for counseling. By his report, she had been in regular and frequently intensive psychotherapy for close to twenty years. Her elaborate psychiatric history included multiple hospitalizations, and she was given to episodes of irrational behavior. The minister, who had recently become the pastor of her church, wanted to get a professional opinion on her mental status and on how much she would ultimately profit from what he was doing with her.

I saw Grace for an assessment interview and came to the conclusion that she was unlikely to change in *any* significant way. As all respectable psychologists can tell you, the best predictor of the future is usually the past. This is not an armchair theoretical opinion but a straightforward empirical principle. If you want to know what someone is going to do today, find out what he or she did yesterday. Was the person irritable or depressed? If so, he or she will probably be irritable or depressed today. There is a demonstrable relationship between present and past, a relationship on which insurance companies rely with great profit—when you hear an insurance representative say on television, as I did last night, "We think drivers who have had accidents or gotten tickets are *more* careful," don't believe it.

Of course, there are exceptions to the past-future rule, but you would not expect a person with a long psychiatric history to be one of them. As far as I could see, the minister might just as well have saved the lady my fee by coming to this conclusion himself. Couldn't he see that if several psychiatrists and psychologists over a twenty-year period were unable to do very much for her; surely *he* would not be able to? Fortunately, he did not see things this way.

Grace had manifested such a wide variety of pathological behaviors, over such an extended length of time, that it was safe to conclude—on the purely human level—that she was a person with serious personality disorganization, and that this disorganization would probably be with her throughout life. Such a person would ordinarily be medicated, and perhaps hospi-talized now and again, but there would be little realistic hope of her ever achieving anything like normal personality integration. Most therapists would have viewed verbal psychotherapy with her as mere maintenance.

I told the minister all this, in softer words, and I believe that I temporarily had him convinced not to look for miracles. Alas, "the harm that good men do"! As one of my clients once told me, a psychologist walks by facts, while a believer walks by faith. Sometimes what one is bold enough to hope for in faith, becomes fact. To get too stuck on "facts," without allowing one's vision to be stretched by faith, is no virtue.

Sometime after I had evaluated Grace, the minister underwent a spiritual renewal that revitalized his Christian walk. He had seen Grace for pastoral counseling on and off throughout this period without much success, but her response to his revitalization was extraordinary. Getting on her knees to pray, she too experienced a transformation, and this had a markedly positive effect on her mental well-being.

As a clinical psychologist with a keen interest in social psychology, I am well acquainted with the magical effects of placebos, positive expectancies, and emotional contagions. Although I cannot prove the accuracy of my opinion, I do not believe that social psychological processes were of much import in Grace's case. At the very least, it must be conceded that *if* her "cure" was just a "hysterical reaction," its quality stands in striking contrast to most of what went on before in her life.

Grace's sudden remission naturally befuddled her husband, whom I never met but who was depicted to me, at the time, as staunchly atheistic and tough minded. Her adult son was equally surprised, and for a while I think the two of them kept expecting her to fall on her face. Even if she does someday—and I doubt this will happen—it would not nullify the years of real health she has already enjoyed. My last report indicated that she was still doing very well indeed.

Returning to the matter of social psychological processes, one might object that Grace received a lot of social support from the Christian church she was attending, and that this support accounted for her success. Surely, whatever support she got helped. But she had been in church before, and frankly, even after her spiritual renewal, she never became a regular attender because of her family's opposition to institutionalized religion. For close to ten years now, she has been living in a remote section of another state, without much Christian companionship.

The psychological changes in Grace would impress a psychotherapist fully as much as a spectacular cancer remission would impress an oncologist. No experienced clinician would have predicted what happened to her. Grace is now, for all intents and purposes, normal.

Maybe her spiritual experience triggered a biochemical correction. If so, that's what I call psychosomatic medicine! Perhaps her normal behavior is merely the playing out of an illusion—the belief that she is healthy. If so, we are talking about a strikingly powerful belief.

Deeper Spiritual Realities. Many people think that "real" therapy occurs only in professionally orthodox ways, under the guidance of a licensed psychologist or psychiatrist. We tend to scoff at spiritual cures, perhaps because we have seen so many false cures, so many fraudulent healings, and so much neurotic emotionalism.

Is it possible that there *is* a devil of some kind, a malevolent intelligence who uses this skepticism of ours to lull us to sleep? "We wrestle not against flesh and blood, but against principalities, against powers, against the ruler of the darkness of this world, against spiritual wickedness in high places."[8]

In earlier chapters, I tried to rough out a picture of how spiritual and psychological processes fit together and interpenetrate. I argued that we ought not to confuse regeneration and psychotherapy, and that we should never reduce one to the other. I presented evidence that psychological health, in the traditional sense of that term, may not always parallel obedience. I attempted to indicate how, in contrast to the claims of some evangelists, commitment to God through Christ does not necessarily result in one's becoming a psychologically healthy person. Just as we cannot routinely expect complete physical healing upon coming to Christ, there is no convincing reason to assume that all our psychological limitations and inadequacies will instantly vanish.

Since part of the mandate of the gospel is to meet human beings where they are and to tend to their wounds, psychotherapy is an eminently legitimate service. What is it, after all, but the systematic healing of the sores of our fellows? The question we are addressing in this chapter is this: Can God, *directly* through his Spirit, in interaction with the human spirit, heal a person psychologically? Does it happen now and again? On the basis of the case I have presented to you—the transformation of Grace—I submit that the answer is yes.

If the general trend of what I am suggesting is correct, what has all this to say to the Christian therapist? Perhaps it implies that psychotherapy should be grounded in faith as well as facts, and that the therapist should continually ask God to make him or her more sensitive to the realm of the Spirit. "We walk by faith and not by sight."

To be a Christian therapist is, at times, an awesome responsibility. If you stop for a moment to appreciate the fact that many, if not the majority, of people who come for therapy are in *some* kind of spiritual crisis, I think you can appreciate the nature of this responsibility. As long as one defines himself or herself as a *Christian* psychotherapist, it will be difficult if not impossible to escape the dual role of pastor and therapist. You can default on this role, but I do not think that you can abolish it.

The important thing to recognize is how hard it is to remain in the tension that is an intrinsic part of this dual role. When *you* are the person on the front lines, with both the clinical and legal responsibility for helping people, it is sometimes very difficult to rely on God. All therapists are trained to "take action," even if this means just offering sincere warmth and understanding. The psychological professions are, understandably, built on the foundational belief that people from their own resources must help other people. There is no explicit provision for faith, and so the battle to maintain it, even in the therapist's psyche, is uphill. In fact, I do not believe that it can be done without the help of the Holy Spirit.

The Diabolical. We began this chapter with a discussion of skepticism, and we have entertained the idea that our battles may in part be spiritual ones. Can any sane and competent therapist take seriously the notion of a devil?

A large number of religious people shirk responsibility for their own faults and failings by blaming them on

Satan. Instead of basking in the love and freedom of
Jesus Christ to "cover all sins," they dwell on trumped-
up projections of their own evil. For years, this made
me so uncomfortable that I could not *say anything*
about the radical nature of evil without feeling acutely
anxious. I could not take seriously the possibility that
there may in fact exist a being who, to use a biblical
metaphor, walks about as a roaring lion "seeking whom
he may devour."[9]

I now treat the whole matter more soberly. Consider
this passage from Lewis's *Screwtape Letters*, in which
Screwtape, a senior devil, is advising young Wormwood
on how to dupe a new Christian:

*I wonder you should ask me whether it is essential to
keep the patient in ignorance of your own existence.
That question, at least for the present phase of the
struggle, has been answered for us by the High
Command. Our policy, for the moment, is to conceal
ourselves. Of course this has not always been so. We are
really faced with a cruel dilemma. When the humans
disbelieve in our existence we lose all the pleasing results
of direct terrorism, and we make no magicians. On the
other hand, when they believe in us, we cannot make
them materialists or skeptics. At least, not yet. I have
great hopes that we shall learn in due time how to
emotionalize and mythologize their science to such an
extent that what is, in effect, a belief in us (though not
under that name) will creep in while the human mind
remains closed to belief in the Enemy. The "Life Force,"
the worship of sex, and some aspects of Psychoanalysis
may prove useful.*

Lewis, a Cambridge and Oxford don, wrote this in the
early 1940s. The paragraph concludes:

*The fact that "devils" are predominantly comic figures in
the modern imagination will help you. If any faint
suspicion of your existence begins to arise in his mind,
suggest to him a picture of something in red tights, and*

persuade him that since he cannot believe in that . . . he therefore cannot believe in you.[10]

Therapy and Ultimate Reality. Even if a person believes neither in an unseen malevolent personality, in an impersonal evil force, nor in any kind of cosmic moral struggle, there is still the question of God. *Is* there an all-powerful Creator who, for unexplained reasons, allows humanity to suffer tremendous pain, yet nevertheless acts *in* the lives of people, so as to woo them toward good and foster their temporal well-being?

Recently I came across a book based on tapes dictated by a dying psychiatrist. Seemingly healthy and vigorous, he discovered in his forties that he had a fatal blood disease. In the months between this discovery and his death, he made the tapes and left them to a writer he knew from their Long Island tennis club. This is what he says, near the end of the book:

Do you know what I'd like most right now, Norman? That is, other than to hear a news bulletin announcing a sudden, new cure for leukemia? I'd like to be able to suspend all reason, shut out entirely the effects of a lifetime of logic. I'd like to be able to believe that just before I finally push off, during those last few moments when I'm half here and half there, that I'll open my eyes for one final look around and see it all, that I'll be able to understand everything wasn't *really just a series of insane accidents, that I didn't just do what I did and love those I loved purely by chance, that I'll finally know there* **was** *a specific plan to it all, a subtle design woven into it with the sure hand of a Master Craftsman—and that even the bad, the terrible, the worst of things were there for some reason, for some better purpose than was ever visible before.*[11]

I can hardly read this without crying. It brings to mind the harsh pathos of life without Christ.[12] All through the book, the psychiatrist describes, in an uncommonly honest way, his failures as a doctor, a father, and a husband. I can identify with him in places. Yet, reading about some of his mistakes, I realize that a Christian therapist might not have made them—not because of any special clinical expertise, but simply because of a certain, often unspoken, set of values.

For example, the dying psychiatrist recognized that he had erred in prompting a passive woman to be assertive, when he did not involve her husband in the treatment, and when he implicitly encouraged her to "stand up for her rights," even if it meant separation. The couple did separate. Then they divorced. She committed suicide. While I greatly respect this doctor for his magnificent honesty, I suspect that a Christian practitioner might have been a little more cautious about shaking up the marriage.

Is there some reason, some unseen purpose to it all? Is there a God who sometimes performs *psychological* miracles? The doctor's tapes are filled with tragic human stories, leading to his final hope that this is so. Christian therapists believe that it is.

NOTES
1. *New English Bible* (New York: Oxford University Press, 1970), p. 3 (Genesis 3:1).
2. *Ibid.,* p. 18 (Matthew 12:30); see also Luke 9:50.
3. Bertrand Russell, *Why I Am Not a Christian* (New York: Simon & Schuster, 1957), pp. 3-23.
4. Bertrand Russell, *Sceptical Essays* (London: Unwin Books, 1935).
5. *Ibid.,* pp. 9-18.
6. See James Daane, *The Freedom of God: A Study of Election and Pulpit* (Grand Rapids: Eerdmans, 1973), p. 116 ff.
7. The proper use of the term "miracle" can be debated. For a helpful technical discussion of the subject, see Geddes MacGregor, *Philosophical Issues in Religious Thought* (Boston: Houghton Mifflin, 1973), pp. 374-388. MacGregor points to the frequent confusion of the magical and the miraculous.
8. Ephesians 6:12 (KJV).
9. 1 Peter 5:8 (KJV).
10. C. S. Lewis, *Screwtape Letters* (New York: Macmillan, 1943/1961), pp. 32, 33.
11. Norman Garbo, *To Love Again: A Psychiatrist's Search for Love* (New York: McGraw-Hill, 1977).
12. The phrase, "pathos of life without Christ," was suggested to me by my college classmate William Devlin.

SIX
EVANGELISM IN
THE CONSULTING ROOM

If there *is* some reason and purpose to it all, and if God *can* and sometimes *does* dramatically intervene in lives —and in the transformation of human personality— Christian therapists may have a duty to tell people so. If patients come to therapists because they want the best help they can get, are Christian therapists justified in applying what may turn out to be Band-Aids in cases where what is needed is radical spiritual surgery?

The Question and Its Context. We have come to an important question. It is actually part of a larger series of issues. Let me frame the question and then relate it to its wider context. I will assume that you agree with my earlier assertions that psychotherapy and regeneration are not identical and that if one had to choose between them, regeneration would have to be given priority.

As a therapist, this puts me in a certain amount of conflict. I am licensed by the state to practice a profession explicitly concerned with helping people by ordinary human means. As we discussed in the last chapter, no room, conceptual or otherwise, is usually reserved for the supernatural, and a fair percentage of the people in my profession might regard any talk of it as very strange indeed. Were such talk to come from an uneducated person, it would simply be seen as superstitious ignorance, but from another psychologist it might be judged more harshly. Many psychologists just do not look kindly on traditional supernaturalism. I add the qualification "traditional" because, as I indicated earlier, some of my colleagues would be more favorably disposed to astrology or extrasensory perception[1] than to New Testament Christianity.

If a therapist can defuse or compartmentalize his or her religious concerns, the problems we are about to explore become less acute. If a particular psychologist, for example, can either regard Christian transformation as less important than therapy, view the two as irrelevant to each other, or believe psychotherapy and regeneration to be the same thing under different labels, this psychologist will probably not feel much conflict from the desire to share Christ with clients. The ethical questions we are going to pose become unimportant or meaningless. They fade into the oblivion of idle philosophizing, or they seem trivial in contrast to the other issues weaving their way through the therapy hour.

Our central question is this: Is it right to discuss the gospel with a psychotherapy client and, if so, under what conditions?

Does it make a difference, for example, whether the client is paying directly for services, or if someone else, such as a government agency, is underwriting the costs of treatment? What about when the therapist is donating the time, either independently or through a church clinic? Is it ethical to relate the gospel to a client, so long as the therapist does so beyond the confines of the treatment hour, say later over a cup of coffee? What about when the therapist is sure it would help alleviate the person's identified problem, perhaps depression or ennui? What if the client is terminally ill or, as a variation on this theme, very old? How about when the client asks the therapist about his or her beliefs? And what of instances when the client asks the therapist, but the latter makes the clinical judgment that encouraging the client in *any* religious ideation might be harmful? Is making such a judgment a form of arrogance?

Present-Future Tensions. There are actually two "contexts" that relate to our main question. First, there is the matter of present-future tension or, to phrase this a little differently, of natural versus spiritual welfare. We discussed this issue in chapters 3 and 4. As a Christian, shall I most concern myself with my brother's or sister's immediate, or ultimate, needs?

Christianity asserts that all persons should be in peaceful relationship with God, through embracing Jesus Christ as Lord and Redeemer. The Holy Spirit's indwelling of believers is a metaphysical reality and not simply a way of speaking about the development of Christian ideas in a person. Heaven and eternal life, together with a universe-wrenching judgment, are also real. On the basis of these beliefs, I take Christian proclamation to be important—not in the sense of "programs" but in the sense of Christians naturally sharing the faith with their neighbors.

At the same time, Christianity instructs us to love others and to tend to their needs, whether for food, clothes, shelter, or simple love. Contrary to media satires, Christianity is not a religion of detachment. Persons who are "so heavenly minded that they are no earthly good" are probably not heavenly minded at all. It rests squarely on the shoulders of Christians to care for the sick, give to the poor and, in general, emulate the model of service shown to us by Jesus.

When these two concerns—the desire to minister to people in their spiritual needs and the desire to care for them materially and psychologically—can be pursued simultaneously, or when there is an orderly progression from one to the other, the tension between the natural and the spiritual largely vanishes. When, however, one must choose *between* the two, between the ultimate and the temporal, one is plunged into conflict.

Consider the medical missionary who spends a great

deal of time helping people with physical problems. Surely everyone would applaud such service. As we shall see when we turn to a consideration of Pauline psychology in the next chapter, one cannot justifiably split the body off from the mind, nor can one ignore the body's ailments in order to cultivate the spirit. A human being is a unified entity. In treating the body one may inevitably affect the spirit.

We will, however, have to take account of what has been termed "Paul's modification of the unitary view of man."[2] Doing medical work is not, in itself, evangelism. To treat the body but neglect the rest of the person is every bit as one-sided as the reverse. Though it may be misguided and ineffective to talk about religion to someone while refusing to mend his or her body, mending the body does not guarantee any mending of the spirit.

What is the proper balance? If the missionary does only medical work and neglects proclamation, perhaps there is no evangelism. If he or she does no medical work, perhaps there is no charity and, as a result, no effective evangelism. What about the missionary doctor who confronts a person on the verge of death? If medically treated with all haste, the person *may* live to hear the good news. If untreated because the doctor is too busy talking about religion, the patient will certainly die.

The Christian psychotherapist, as far as I can see, is in much the same position as the missionary. Out of compassion for others, he or she extends to them all the healing nourishment possible. At the same time, believing the client's eternal welfare to be of paramount importance, it is difficult for the Christian clinician to put aside concerns relating to faith.

As we have already noted, the practice of psycho-therapy is intrinsically noble, and its worth need not be established by anything else. Just as the medical missionary need not argue that medicine is valuable *because* it can be made part of the process of sharing the Christian faith with people, the therapist need not argue the value of therapy by appealing to its possible evangelistic uses. Nevertheless, a Christian therapist is going to be motivated to introduce others to Christ, especially since so much of the work of the therapist directly addresses itself to the hurts, needs, and longings of persons—precisely those things to which Christianity itself is addressed. The Christian therapist is thus always potentially caught in the present-future or ultimate-penultimate agony.

Undue Influence. The other context of our question is the extent to which members of the psychological helping professions should be allowed to tamper with patients' beliefs. This concern relates to all therapists, whether religious or not. Does *any* therapist have the right, and possibly the responsibility, to change what a client believes?

That therapists do this is well documented,[3] and a moment's reflection will suggest that many people seek therapy for the specific purpose of altering beliefs. Consider the patient who wants his or her feelings of hopelessness treated. The "feeling" of no hope is often undergirded by a set of unfortunate beliefs.

Think of the bankrupt individual—no hope!—who suddenly inherits a large fortune. For such a person, beliefs about the future have quite a bit to do with mood states. The belief that money will soon be available brings hope. It probably also lifts depression!

How far therapists should go in trying to change clients' beliefs relates to: the *kinds* of beliefs at issue (religious beliefs may be in a different category than, say, beliefs about one's personal attractiveness); whether the client has given *informed consent* for their alteration; and to the degree to which the *community* at large would judge them as pathogenic (e.g., in *this* culture paranoid beliefs are judged undesirable).

These three ways to evaluate the legitimacy of altering beliefs do not fully resolve our ethical question, however, since each is by nature subjective. Recall our discussion of basic premises in chapter 1. Somehow we have to decide how to categorize beliefs; but this involves our beliefs about beliefs. Someone, whether the clinician or the court, has to determine if the client gave truly informed consent, a judgment that comes down to a belief. Finally, the community is made up of people whose beliefs are not infallible (e.g., Nazis). How much society allows therapists to alter clients' *religious* beliefs ultimately hinges on public opinion.

Under a theocratic government, such as the one that existed in Salem during the early seventeenth century, strong religious "persuasion" would be normative. Under an antireligious totalitarian regime, such as the one that now exists in Russia, little or no religious persuasion or encouragement would be tolerated. In an age of general religious tolerance and church-state separation such as we currently enjoy in America, therapists probably have substantial, although certainly not absolute, discretionary power. The ethical question is not what therapists can get away with, however, but what they should do. What is right?

Germane to our discussion of therapists influencing clients' religious beliefs is what I call coercive persuasion —the use of inordinate power to modify attitudes. Legal scholars talk about duress when power or the threat of power is used to get people to do something they would not otherwise do.

Coercive persuasion in therapy is not duress in the usual sense. It consists of gradual alterations —"shapings"—of beliefs, by means of what has traditionally been called transference. Because the power that a client gives a therapist is like the power of a parent over a child, the therapist does seem more able than most people to alter the client's beliefs. Naturally, when a belief is clearly destructive to a patient,—e.g., "I believe I ought to jump out of that ten-story window"—it would be an unusual therapist who places some abstract notion of the patient's freedom[4] above the latter's concrete welfare. Still, the question of freedom, freedom of belief and freedom of choice, remains.

One could question the assumption that psycho-therapists enjoy all that much persuasive power. I once spent the better part of a day chatting with Kenneth Colby, a very well known and well regarded psychiatrist at UCLA. He remarked that one thing therapists seem *unable* to alter is patients' major beliefs. Colby is a leading expert on paranoid process and is, therefore, well qualified to render an opinion about the modification of beliefs.

Seymour Halleck, another eminent psychiatrist, was invited to write a response to a case report we will presently review. Halleck says in this response, "It has been my impression that consumers who have free choice of therapists . . . tend to seek help from therapists who share their belief systems."[5] Psychologist Donald Tweedie also doubts that therapists can do very much to impress their beliefs on patients.[6]

I have no doubt that frontal assaults on a patient's beliefs, especially if these are strongly held, would meet with considerable resistance. Social psychologists have spoken of the "reactance" phenomenon. Try to control someone and you push all kinds of buttons prompting this person to counter your efforts. More subtle forms of attitude modification might be more successful, however, apart from whether the therapist intends them to be. Faith, or the lack of it, is not always set in mental cement. It can be affected by life events on a day-to-day basis. Since most persons who come to therapy are demoralized,[7] it is not hard to allow that religious attitudes are capable of being influenced.

But the sword of persuasion cuts both ways. Remember that our principal concern in this chapter is the rightness or wrongness of a *Christian* therapist telling clients about the Christian faith. Is it ethical to "evangelize" clients?

Tweedie has an interesting answer.[8] He makes a distinction between imposition and exposition and argues that, while the Christian therapist should not *impose* beliefs *on* clients, he or she can certainly *expose* beliefs *to* clients. This formulation has much to recommend it, so long as we acknowledge that the imposition-exposition distinction may be easier to draw on paper than to put into practice.

The Case of Mary. I want to explore these issues further by considering an article[9] that appeared in a leading American Psychological Association journal.[10] It had to do with the diagnosis and treatment of a twenty-eight-year-old Christian Science mother, who showed an array of phobic and obsessive symptoms. Mary was "afraid of everything," including many animals and diseases, such as botulism and tetanus. Psychotherapy was initiated when she came to an emergency room at 3:00 A.M., requesting that her young son, who had been knocked down by a dog the previous afternoon, be treated for rabies. Although she knew that rabies could not be contracted through simple contact with the dog's paws, this "knowledge" did not allay her fear of the disease. Mary's phobic obsessionalism was so pervasive that she became almost bizarrely fastidious in her eating habits, and she would rush to the doctor to demand a tetanus injection if she so much as pricked her finger. She also had trouble sleeping and, out of concern for the health of her family, had quit her job.

Mary had been introduced to Christian Science by her husband. Over the years she had used Christian Science procedures several times, for example, to ameliorate the pain of her first childbirth. This particular application turned out badly, though, in that she still experienced a painful labor and delivery. Later incidents, such as the death of a devout practitioner who had refused medical treatment, reinforced Mary's doubt toward the Christian Science doctrine of "mind over matter." These episodes, coupled with her own questions about the nature of God and the problem of evil, resulted in "harsh disillusionment." She stopped attending Christian Science services.

Prior to the onset of the severe obsessions which brought her to therapy, Mary suffered a miscarriage. She also reported three experiences during the pregnancy that presumably rekindled her interest in Christian Science. First, a friend developed multiple sclerosis and Mary found herself comforting the woman through prayer. Second, her three-year-old son showed a complete remission of nocturnal foot pain after a practitioner, at Mary's request, prayed for the boy. Third, Mary may have contributed to her miscarriage, in that she had helped move some heavy furniture during pregnancy. Since she did not want the baby to begin with, Mary felt that somehow she had killed the fetus "by thought." This chain of events left her with considerable guilt.

The central argument in the case report is that Mary, through her involvement in Christian Science, became sensitized to her own cognitive processes, such that she began "tuning in on disaster." Reinforcing this sensitization were memories of several experiences in her past that lent validity to the Christian Science thesis, including the fact that she had been able to end a heavy smoking habit through the use of Christian Science thought control procedures. The writers of the case history argue that when Mary spontaneously, but reluctantly, brought up her involvement with Christian Science, "a probable basis for her obsessive behavior became clear."[11]

During her therapy, Mary was given relaxation training to enable her to cope better with her daily anxieties and her insomnia, and she was taught a standard thought-stopping procedure to use when she found herself obsessing. Her interest in Christian Science dwindled, as did her obsessionalism. Mary returned to work and, at her three-months' follow up, was continuing to "do quite well."[12]

There are a number of critical issues here. First, have the authors proved their argument? *Was* Christian Science of etiological significance in the onset of Mary's psychological disorder?

Because of the nature of a case report, specifically the fact that many sources of influences on the person under study are neither controlled nor accounted for, one can rarely establish definite causation.[13] There is always the danger of the *post hoc, ergo propter hoc* fallacy, i.e., because B follows A, one concludes that A had to cause B.

For the benefit of readers who may be interested in the logic of behavioral science methods,[14] this is the trouble with all *"ex post facto"* research. An *ex post facto* study is one in which the researcher, instead of controlling what happens, simply observes what has already happened. One cannot infer causation from correlation. The number of drownings on a particular day can be predicted reasonably well on the basis of knowing the amount of ice cream sold on the previous day. Obviously, people do not drown because they eat too much ice cream. Hot weather "causes" both the sale of ice cream and the use of the beaches, which, of course, provides the occasion for drowning.

As I examine the case report on Mary, I must concede that her involvement with Christian Science may have played a role in the development of her difficulties. This is not certain, however, and it could have been the other way around. Her fears and obsessions might have augmented her interest in Christian Science. Any honest clinician will have to admit, nonetheless, that religious ideation may, at times, be pathogenic. At very least, it can serve as a vehicle for the expression of psycho-pathology.

A second issue has to do with whether "religion" and "Christian Science" are interchangeable terms. Perhaps because of her limited religious experience, Mary seemed to think they were, and so did the doctors who reported the case. They seemed unaware of the fact that, when Mary's interest in Christian Science was rekindled, this might simply have reflected a more general upsurge of interest in religion. Mary and her therapist—to use the cliché once more—*may* have discarded the baby with the bath water. In rejecting the particular religion of Christian Science, Mary may have unwittingly rejected a much broader class of phenomena, i.e., all religion.

The third issue concerns the possibility that Mary's religiosity was more functional than her doctors realized. Given that her husband introduced her to Christian Science, might this religion have played some positive role in their marriage? Note also that Mary was able to stop smoking by using Christian Science methods. Given that the regular inhalation of cigarette smoke is demonstrably carcinogenic, her religious techniques may have saved her life.

A colleague and I published a more extended analysis of this case which may be consulted for further details.[15] Our concern here is the question of whether Mary's therapist had the right to deal with her *religious* beliefs. The general form of the question is:

If it can be ascertained that religious beliefs are sometimes of etiological significance in the onset of psychopathology, does a psychotherapist have the right, and possibly the responsibility, to combat such beliefs in any situation in which he or she deems them to be perpetuating psychological disturbance?[16]

In our extended analysis, we suggest that therapists may often disabuse people of cherished beliefs unintentionally. We also suggest that, in certain instances, the therapist may indeed have to root out psychopathological religiosity. However, modesty and caution in forming judgments of exactly what *is* pathological are extremely important when dealing with religion. Otherwise, the therapist potentially puts himself or herself over God.

Church-State Issues. Another reason for exercising modesty and caution is the crucial importance of maintaining the separation of church and state. Attacking even patently bizarre religious beliefs may ultimately have negative implications for the preservation of civil liberties. Eventually any belief system, say Christianity, could be labeled bizarre. Taken to extremes, the earnest maintenance of a theistic belief might constitute grounds for refusing to grant a license to an otherwise qualified psychologist.

To illustrate that this concern is not overdrawn,

the Graduate School of Psychology at Fuller Theological
Seminary, where I teach, has been extensively scrutinized and site-visited by the American Psychological
Association for the specific purpose of determining
if our religious beliefs and practices adversely affect
our ability to train competent clinical psychologists.
For years, the doctoral psychology program at Fuller
was one of only about a hundred approved by the
Association, and one of only four in the State of
California so approved (the others being Berkeley, USC,
and UCLA). In some states, there is an intimate
connection between licensing and whether or not a
psychologist's training was completed in APA-approved
settings.

Ethics and Urgency. What about simply relating the
basic Christian ideas to a therapy patient? Unless the
patient has come to the therapist to hear such ideas, is
it unethical to use time expressly committed to another
purpose even for this? And yet, if there is urgency to the
situation. . . .

Is there not always urgency? Is not the Christian
therapist treating an unbeliever in the position of
possibly talking to a dying man or woman? What of the
rules? What of the ethics? Did not Jesus himself break
the rules? How is the Christian therapist to know when,
and when not, to talk about God?

The issue is comparatively simple when the client
directly asks about the therapist's beliefs, assuming that
the inquiry is not a way to throw the therapist off the
track. If the question is genuine, the therapist may be
doing no one a service by dodging it.

Complications do arise, however. Some clients may be
sincerely interested in the therapist's religion, but their
interest may stem from a desire to copy the therapist in
any way possible, or to make the therapist's beliefs part
of their defense system.

In these cases, the therapist may be in the same
position as one is with a child (note our above reference
to transference). Given how children, or patients,

sometimes distort what they hear, the therapist has to be vigilant to see, in advance, the implications of talking, *or refusing to talk*, about God. Does the therapist not change hats when he or she starts to talk about faith?

Perry London, in a response he wrote to the case report on Mary, applauds its authors for opening up one more taboo topic, "one more normative Pandora's box."[17] He advocates the bold confrontation of anything a therapist judges to be religious neurosis. I believe his advice to be a bit cavalier. Turning the problem around, however, does the unbelieving client not have a right to be protected from religiously zealous mental health practitioners?

We have not yet touched on whether Christianity can and should be used as a specific treatment, perhaps for clients who complain that they find life meaningless. This raises a criterion problem. A particular therapist might come to believe that all of his or her clients suffer from meaninglessness.

Consider the work of Viktor Frankl,[18] who is not a Christian, but who nevertheless views lack of meaning as *the* key psychiatric malady. One could argue, as Donald Tweedie does, that practically everyone seeking therapy is in search of a philosophy. Since therapists may provide one, whether they intend to or not, why not do so explicitly and deliberately? Why *not* offer Christianity?

I believe, nonetheless, the *client's* responsibility for personal existential decisions must be cultivated. While it may be desirable for a therapist to inform prospective clients about his or her religious beliefs, *all* therapists, religious or not, must respect the client's freedom and facilitate the client's autonomous existential choices.

Between the Hammer and the Anvil. Sometimes I feel caught between the hammer of the state and the anvil of the Spirit. One is the protector of individual freedom, and the other is the regenerator of persons. An especially helpful discussion of how the two relate appears in John Murray's *Problem of Religious Freedom.*[19]

Murray discusses two views of what has been called the "care of religion by the state." The first is that only truth has rights and, thus, while "error" may be tolerated it is never given legal authorization. There is personal freedom of belief, including worship within the family, but error has no right to public propagation (although, in certain countries where religious pluralism exists, "erroneous" worship may be allowed so as to maintain the public peace). The other view does not operate in terms of mere toleration but takes a more serious view of religious freedom *per se.* Self-determination by the individual is primary.

The problem of religious freedom is closely related to the problem of whether individual therapists have the right to persuade clients along religious lines. Therapists, by virtue of the fact that they are licensed, act as *de facto* agents of the secular state. Does the government have the right to prohibit therapists from religious persuasion? Does it have the right to insist that *its* religion—whatever this may be, for example, materialism, selfism, or some other secularism—be implicitly or explicitly propagated by the Christian psychotherapist?

A Practical Answer. My own answer to our ethical question—and this answer is still evolving—is to be as explicit as I can about what I believe, and also to be as open as I can to discuss philosophic and religious issues when clients raise them and when these issues, in my judgment, are genuine existential concerns.

A few years out of graduate school, I became acutely uncomfortable because I was practicing in an office that belonged to another psychologist who was not especially interested in religious matters and whose suites, therefore, had nothing about them to suggest that anyone working there was willing to discuss philosophic-theologic questions. While I wanted to let clients know my position, I could never find a way to do this without feeling intrusive.

A few of my clients seemed to be struggling hard to

find a coherent world view, a way to give ultimate meaning to human living. Suddenly launching into a presentation of *my* world did not seem to be congruent with the role of the therapist as I conceived it. The furthest I ever went was to give someone a copy of C. S. Lewis's *Mere Christianity,* and that for me felt like going pretty far.

My eventual solution was to move out of those suites into an office of my own. Since the other practitioners working in my new location were believers, we were able to put the word "Christian" on the office door and in the telephone book. Everyone coming to us knew at least the general nature of our beliefs. Curiously enough, we found that a fair number of avowed agnostics and atheists came for consultation. Christianity, instead of scaring them off, seemed to offer them a certain comfort, perhaps the reassurance that they would be seen by someone who was "safe" and not likely to be caught up in the latest Southern California fad or fashion. Maybe people also came because they wanted to be around someone with a coherent world view.

This way of practicing seemed to augment informed consent. Clients coming through the door knew where we stood, and so did not have to worry about any surprises months down the line. Sometimes a person reads a book written by a psychotherapist and then seeks out this therapist because he or she likes the therapist's ideas about treatment. In our case, clients may have sought us out because they liked our philosophy of life. They seemed to think, quite correctly, that our beliefs had something to do with the way we practiced.

Now that I teach at a theological seminary, my religious beliefs are even more explicit, since a person who wants to know them in outline has only to look through the seminary catalog. While it is true that only a small number of Christian therapists work in such a setting, it is certainly possible for *any* psychotherapist to prepare a brief written statement of beliefs for distribution to prospective clients. Such a statement could also include other important kinds of information, for example, educational background, professional experience, credentials held, and therapeutic orientation (e. g., "Rogerian" or "Behavioral"). This kind of truth-in-packaging by Christian practitioners could well set a standard to be emulated by all mental health professionals.

In the next chapter we will turn our attention to a different but related set of issues. When we discussed the relationship between ultimate and temporal good, we briefly referred to the view of personality reflected through the writings of the Apostle Paul. The Bible was written over a long period of time by many different people, and it is possible to find statements about the nature of the human person all through it. Paul's statements, however, are the most complete. We will now examine them.

NOTES
1. I probably take some liberties here in calling these forms of supernaturalism, but perhaps the point I am making will stand anyway.
2. See George Eldon Ladd, *A Theology of the New Testament* (Grand Rapids: Eerdmans, 1974), pp. 463, 464.
3. See Perry London, *The Modes and Morals of Psychotherapy* (New York: Holt, Rinehart & Winston, 1964).
4. Freedom is a notoriously ambiguous concept.
5. Seymour L. Halleck, "Discussion of 'Socially Reinforced Obsessing,'" *Journal of Consulting and Clinical Psychology*, XLIV (February 1976), pp. 146-147.
6. Donald F. Tweedie, Jr., "Psychology, Faith, and Values: A Christian Comment," in *Psychology and Faith: The Christian Experience of Eighteen Psychologists*, ed. by H. Newton Malony (unpublished).
7. Jerome Frank, another dean of American psychiatry, greatly stresses this point.
8. Donald F. Tweedie, Jr., "Psychology, Faith, and Values."
9. Ronald Jay Cohen and Frederick J. Smith, "Socially Reinforced Obsession: Etiology of a Disorder in a Christian Scientist," *Journal of Consulting and Clinical Psychology*, XLIV (February 1976), pp. 142-144.
10. Journals published by the American Psychological Association, of which there are about fifteen, tend to be regarded as the best in the field.

11. Cohen and Smith, "Socially Reinforced Obsession," p. 144.
12. *Ibid.*
13. I say "rarely" rather than "never" because in some cases causation *is* clear. Consider mental retardation resulting from head trauma in a previously normal person.
14. Technically, *all* research suffers from this defect, in that even well-controlled experiments "affirm the consequent."
15. Clinton W. McLemore and John Court, "Religion and Psychotherapy: Ethics, Civil Liberties, and Clinical Savvy—a Critique," *Journal of Consulting and Clinical Psychology,* XLV (December 1977), pp. 1172-1175.
16. This statement of the question is perhaps faulty. "Situation" might better be modified by "psychotherapeutic" and after "onset" should probably appear "and continuance." Also, this is obviously not the most general form of the question, and it is not the key ethical question around which the chapter is centered, which has to do with what Christian therapists ought to do.
17. Perry London, "Psychotherapy for Religious Neurosis? Comments on Cohen and Smith," *Journal of Consulting and Clinical Psychology,* XLIV (February 1976), p. 146.
18. Viktor E. Frankl, *Man's Search for Meaning: An Introduction to Logotherapy* (New York: Washington Square Press, 1963).
19. John Courtney Murray, *The Problem of Religious Freedom* (Westminster, Md.: Newman Press, 1965). Although the second of the book's three chapters is a documentation of papal statements and is, thus, tangential to the Protestant tradition, the other two chapters are very instructive and entirely relevant to our topic. Murray draws distinctions, for example, between proselytism and evangelism, and between the state and society.

SEVEN
PERSONALITY THEORY AND PAULINE PSYCHOLOGY

Nearly all methods of psychotherapy derive from or at least are rationalized by a theory of personality. Sigmund Freud, for example, conceived of human personality as largely the expression of conflict and its resolution. The Id, present from birth, is said in the Freudian psychology to be the repository of primitive impulses that continually cry out for gratification. The Superego, a later development, consists of the conscience and the ego ideal which together reflect the introjected (taken in) values of the family and society. The Ego, which serves as the executor of the personality, has the difficult job of keeping the peace among the Id, the Superego, and the outside world. Society, of course, rewards conformity but punishes rebellion.

The Freudian technique of therapy involves bringing unconscious material into consciousness, on the assumption that awareness—"insight"—defuses intrapsychic tensions. Other therapists, for example Carl Rogers or Alfred Adler, published alternative conceptions of personality that relate directly to the procedures each defined as therapeutic.

The Nature of the Question. Much of the content of traditional personality theories is hard to prove or disprove. This is one reason why there are so many different theories in the professional marketplace. Most of them are long on *clinical philosophy* and short on *scientifically testable* content. They are heavily colored with metaphysical and ethical ideas that, as we have seen repeatedly, by their nature are not capable of empirical verification. For a psychological construct to be even minimally scientific, it must be defined by objective observations that any reasonably intelligent person could be trained to make.

The Christian psychotherapist naturally wonders if Scripture contains a theory of personality. On the surface of things, this does not seem like an unreasonable possibility, since there are many statements in the Bible about the nature of the person. If one studies the Bible carefully enough, can one put together a view of personality that has as much, if not more, *clinical* utility than the traditional psychological theories?

Exactly how far does the Bible go in providing us with a rigorous "anthropology," as theologians like to call it? Should we view Freud, Jung, Adler, Sullivan, Horney, Fromm, Erikson, Maslow, Allport, Rogers, Leary, Murray, Sheldon, Lewin, Kelly, May, and Skinner as theological usurpers? If Christian therapists truly want to help people, are they best advised to clear their heads of conventional psychological ideas and to study only Holy Writ?

Does Scripture reveal everything of importance about our inner workings and about the intricacies of human social behavior, or does it have mostly to do with our dealings with and dispositions toward God? Does Scripture detail the structure of our everyday thoughts, feelings, and behaviors, or does it primarily depict our commerce with the transcendent? Can we deduce from Scripture not only the basic nature of a human being but the fundamental principles that inform our everyday behavior as well?

I have heard it said that there is no Christian *perspective* on personality and that theology rightly concerns itself only with spiritual matters, which have little to do with the ordinary workings of personality. On the weight of Scripture, I cannot see how this could be true.

Surely walking in the Spirit must, in the long run, affect one's personality, if for no other reason than that acting in a certain way eventually pulls one's internal tendencies in the same direction, at least if the action is not perceived as having been coerced by outside agents.[1] Christian transformation *must* have some temporal implications, although, as I have tried to show in earlier chapters, specifying these implications is not easy.

Even if we clearly understand how the spiritual can and does inform the natural, this would not necessarily give us a *theory* of personality in the sense in which psychologists customarily use that term. We might know about how faith affects behavior but we would not necessarily know about the basic workings of the personality on which the Spirit operates. We would know about people in relation to God. I am not sure we would know much about people in relation to other people, although as John reminds us in his first epistle, the two spheres are certainly related.

To do justice to our subject, we must examine what Scripture says about human psychology. An especially helpful source is George Ladd's text on biblical theology, since Ladd devotes an entire chapter to the Pauline view of personality.[2] Following the outline of Ladd's chapter, we will explore first the Old Testament uses of *nephesh* (soul), *basar* (flesh), and *ruach* (spirit), and then the New Testament uses of *psychē* (soul), *pneuma* (spirit), *sōma* (body), *sarx* (flesh), *kardia* (heart), *nous* (mind), *ho esō anthrōpos* (the inner man), and *syneidēsis* (conscience). It is obvious that Paul used many different terms in discussing the nature of the human person.

Soul, Flesh, and Spirit in the Old Testament. The Hebrew view of the person differs somewhat from the Greek view. It should be noted, however, in the interests of accuracy, that late Hebrew thought was substantially hellenized and that the sharp distinction that has often been drawn between Greek and Hebrew thought is mistaken.

In the Old Testament, body and soul seem not to stand in contrast to each other. *Basar* is used to designate the body and to underscore human frailty. "Body and the divine breath together make the vital, active *nephesh*,"[3] or soul. Eventually soul comes to signify the human being as a total entity.

The word for spirit (*ruach*), which derived from the idea of air in motion, is often used of God, particularly to designate his power at work in the world, creating and sustaining life. Man's spirit comes from God's spirit. It should be noted that while soul was generally used to indicate the person in relation to other human beings, spirit was usually used to indicate the person in relation to God. Neither was highlighted as a part of the person surviving the death of the body.

In the literature written between the two testaments, *pneuma* (spirit) and *psychē* (soul) come to stand for entities capable of separate existences. In fact, the two terms are sometimes used interchangeably, their preexistence is suggested, and *pneuma* begins to be used of supernatural spirits, both good and bad, and of the person, without implication of derivation from God's spirit.

The modern term "psychology" comes, of course, from *psychē*, not from *pneuma*. Psychology, as we know it today, focuses on person-person events and processes, not on the God-person relationship.

Soul, Spirit, and Body in the New Testament. Turning to the New Testament, Paul uses soul (*psychē*) in a manner that is closer to the Old Testament usage than to that in the intertestamental literature. Nowhere does Paul speak of the soul as a separate entity, or as capable of surviving the death of the body. And he does not write of the salvation of the soul. In contrast with the Old Testament writers, however, Paul fixes his attention on spirit (*pneuma*).

All people, not just Christians, are characterized by spirit. This is what allows even unbelievers to enjoy *human* relationships. The "quickening" of our spirits by God's Spirit is what allows us to enter into a living relationship with him.

Spirit seems to refer to an inner dimension of the person. Since divine life can be imparted to us even while our bodies are perishing, the spiritual dimension is obviously different from the bodily dimension. We should also note that spirit is differentiated from mind and that it often carries with it a strong affective connotation. Perhaps, as I intimated earlier, God reaches us partly through our emotions. Perhaps without changed feelings it is impossible to become a Christian!

Regarding the body (*sōma*) itself, from 1 Corinthians 15 it is clear that Christians are to inherit a real, though different, body. Salvation is not just of the spirit or soul—it is of the body as well.

Flesh and Three Modes of Life. Paul uses another word, *sarx* (flesh), that is of great importance. This term is employed in many ways, for example to refer to bodily tissues and to outward appearances, but of primary significance is Paul's "ethical use of *sarx.*" In this usage, "man as flesh is contrasted with Spirit, is sinful, and without the aid of the Spirit cannot please God."[4]

What has psychology to do with this? From the trichotomy depicted in 1 Corinthians 2:14 to 3:3, where Paul refers to *psychikos* (the natural person), *sarkikos* (the fleshly person) and *pneumatikos* (the spiritual person), it appears that psychology as we know it is largely concerned with *psychikos.* Clinical psychology and related disciplines seem to shed additional light on the nature of *sarx.*

Heart, Mind, the Inner Person, and Conscience. The Greek word for heart (*kardia*) is essentially the same as the Hebrew word for heart (*lēb*). As one might expect, heart is more or less the seat of the emotions. The Greek word *kardia*, however, is used in a number of ways—to

refer to intellectual activity, will, and ethical judgment—
and thus it has no single meaning. Ladd writes, it
"designates the inner life of man from various points of
view."[5]

The Greek word for mind (*nous*) is also used in several
ways. When Paul uses *nous*, he most often means
practical judgment, including everyday understanding
and moral discernment, particularly as this conditions
our intents and behaviors.

When Paul refers to the inner person (*ho esō
anthrōpos*), he is designating "the higher, essential self,
either redeemed or redeemable, made for God and
opposed to sin."[6] Conscience (*syneidēsis*), which has
no Hebrew equivalent except perhaps for *lēb* (heart), is
that which allows us to make moral judgments. It is not,
however, an autonomous guide. The Christian
conscience must be informed by the Holy Spirit, and for
the unbeliever conscience is even less of a trustworthy
guide.

Personality Theory and the Pauline Perspective. How
does the Pauline psychology stack up as a personality
theory, when it is viewed through the lenses of
contemporary behavioral science? Do the Pauline terms
have clear referents and are they used in consistent,
nonoverlapping ways? If they do overlap in meaning, is
it evident which are the subordinate and which the
superordinate constructs? Does the Pauline psychology
lead to definite behavioral predictions and, if so, do
the predictions lend themselves to unambiguous
empirical testing? Is the system concise? And are the
constructs themselves potentially measurable?[7]

Against the backdrop of these questions, it seems
clear that the Pauline material, like the traditional
theories of personality in psychology, is more
philosophical than scientific. It is more of the nature of
an introductory framework for psychology than of a
psychological science. Evaluating Paul's conceptions as
if they were a detailed, empirically oriented theory of
personality, therefore, is inappropriate. Paul is primarily

concerned with spiritual matters, not with natural protoplasmic functioning.

It may be that Paul's writings tell us what we most need to know about people along ontological and ethical lines, but that the rest of it—people as people, and people with people—has been left pretty much to our discovery. The natural structures and processes of personality are the principal concerns of the psychology of personality as we know it. These are what all the great personality theorists try to elucidate, however much they may try, here and there, to smuggle in philosophical contraband. Paul's epistles simply give us a skeleton that contemporary psychology will have to flesh out.

Three Problematical Attempts. We will now briefly examine some ideas from three traditional personality theories. Later we will devote two entire chapters to an examination of psychotherapy methods and the conceptions of human personality that inform them. Here, I will simply demonstrate how a thinking Christian might go about sifting from a personality theory those aspects that are, by nature, philosophical rather than scientific. We will consider Freud because his theory is the most comprehensive and best known, Maslow because his ideas are the ideological framework for "humanistic psychology," and Fromm because he was uncommonly honest about his theoretical activities.

Freud's psychoanalytic theory stresses intrapsychic conflict and the specific ways that people try to reconcile three warring forces: innate needs for sexual and aggressive discharge; prohibitions of conscience; and the external world, which tends to punish imprudence. Among Freud's greatest contributions was his elaborate detailing of the lengths to which people go to avoid honestly facing themselves. Freud is also well known for his psychosexual stages of development.[8] His most controversial formulation was the theory of libido, presumably a psychic energy of sexual origin that Freud took to be the great dynamo of personality. Without going into Freud's important therapeutic ideas, for example, his notion of transference, let us briefly note how this small sampling of Freudian material may look under the light of Christian theology.

That sex and aggression are always the ultimate motives behind human behavior has been denied by many later theorists, for example, Harry Stack Sullivan, Karen Horney, and Carl Rogers. Although sexual and aggressive impulses often seem central to *sarx* (flesh) in its ethical usage, from the Christian perspective it seems that the denial of one's proper creaturehood, along with rebellion against God, is the cardinal motive in the natural person[9]—though certainly one's biological needs may be momentarily prepotent. There is also considerable debate over whether aggression is, in fact, a biological need in human beings.

Freud viewed conscience as entirely derivative. What a person judges to be right or wrong is, according to Freud, totally the result of internalizing others' values, for example the values of parents and teachers. Freud leaves no room for any inherent sense of right and wrong or for any healthy tendency to make ethical judgments. While the Christian psychologist admits the large extent to which standards of conscience may be molded by experience, he or she wants to retain the assumption that we are, by nature, valuing beings. The Christian believes that all people have at least some inkling of God's Law, regardless of cultural context.

So what Freud thought was basic—sex and aggression —may not be so basic after all, and Freud may have missed the fundamental fact that people are intrinsically oriented toward, and capable of making, genuine ethical judgments. Note that Freud was not necessarily wrong in his ideas about how people handle their impulses, but he was not getting to the essence of many human problems. This essence is often a spiritual one.

Turning to Abraham Maslow, he emphasized positive instead of negative qualities in the human person. He was asset rather than liability oriented, more interested in attributes of health than of illness. Selecting only two of Maslow's ideas for discussion, he writes that people are inherently growth oriented and, like Carl Rogers, he criticizes the "sin and sickness" mindset. Maslow was tired of hearing about badness and deficiency. He wanted psychologists to take a more positive view.

His other important idea is that before a person can pursue "higher needs," such as ethics and aesthetics, the person must first get all the lower needs satisfied, for example, needs for food, shelter, security, sex, and love.

Maslow's focus on growth, and on our inherent tendency toward it, seems at times to trivialize the nature of evil as well as the Christian idea of fallen nature. Both become simple developmental failures, the results of adverse but basically innocent psychological and social conditions. As far as our having to have lower needs met before we can pursue higher ones, there is obviously some truth to this. A starving person is unlikely to spend very much time in art galleries. At the same time, if our need for God is classified as a "higher" need—a classification we might question—I wonder how many of us would ever have become Christians. Some people seem most open to God when they are most desperate.

Finally, let us take note of Erich Fromm. I want to discuss him even though he did not offer a highly developed theory of personality. He is important to our discussion because he was honest in admitting that his concerns were expressly philosophical. Like the existential psychologists, Fromm highlighted the importance of unprovable postulates, both in living and in psychotherapy. He was candid in saying that he was explicitly interested in philosophical questions, and he made no pretense of being thoroughly scientific. Because of his candor, some of his more questionable ideas are easy to identify.

He tells us, for example, that the ultimate guide to human conduct is psychological health. What is healthy is good. Since we have had occasion to explore this line of thinking before (see chapter 4), I will not belabor it here. But I do want to point out the Alice in Wonderland quality to it. Recall that, in response to Alice's inquiry, Humpty Dumpty says in *Through the Looking Glass and What Alice Found There:* "When I use a word, it means just what I choose it to mean—neither more nor less. The question is which is to be the master —that's all." What is goodness? Health. What is health? Whatever I say it is. Such circularity plunges us into the abyss of the arbitrary.

I tried to show earlier that the New Testament writers did not intend or pretend to give us a scientific theory of personality. Even the intricacies of Paul's writings do not provide detailed and precise predictions of human behavior in specific everyday situations. They do, however, inform us of our standing, or lack of standing, with God. Paul focused his anthropological thought on the dynamics of regeneration, on transformation in Christ. He did not try to do the work of the modern psychologist or psychotherapist. Indeed, psychology and psychotherapy, as we know them, were as unknown in Paul's time as microbiology or nuclear physics.

That there is no science of personality to be found in the Bible is precisely what one would expect, since neither does the Bible contain information about microbes or mesons. The fact that most modern psychological theories of personality are nearly as bereft of rigorous science is a bit harder to understand. This fact may reflect two others—that behavioral science, by its nature, cannot fully comprehend the human spirit, and that clinicians such as Freud, knowingly or unknowingly, felt a strong need to do so. We turn now to a consideration of the human spirit.

NOTES
1. I am thinking here both of cognitive dissonance research and of behavior therapist folklore. Please note that I am not intending this as a total explanation of the fruits of the Spirit.
2. George Eldon Ladd, "The Pauline Psychology," *A Theology of the New Testament* (Grand Rapids: Eerdmans, 1974), pp. 457-478. Ladd also provides a list of other relevant writings.
3. *Ibid.,* p. 458.

4. *Ibid.,* p. 469.
5. *Ibid.,* p. 475.
6. *Ibid.,* p. 477.
7. I might point out, in passing, that even most mainline theories of personality do not come out very well on these dimensions. Why? Because they, too, are more suggestive and philosophical than definitive and psychological.
8. The psychosexual stages, principally oral, anal, phallic, latent, and genital.
9. I here neglect the idea of outside agents—devils—which are said to play a role in this rebellion. See chapter 5.

EIGHT
PSYCHOTHERAPY, SPIRIT, AND THE MYSTICAL

As I tried to show in the preceding chapter, there is no biblical theory of personality, at least none that stands as an alternative to those contemporary psychological theories that treat complex clinical phenomena. The Bible concerns itself more with the dynamics of faith than with everyday intrapsychic processes. Scripture does, however, describe an aspect of personality that is of critical importance in day-to-day psychological functioning, whether we are viewing this functioning through the lenses of theology *or* psychology. This aspect is spirit.

A psychotherapist who is oblivious to the spiritual nature of personality is in the position of a medical doctor who, in performing a physical examination, neglects to examine the patient's heart. The psychologist who has most explicitly discussed the human spirit in psychotherapy is John G. Finch. In his doctoral dissertation,[1] he scrutinized the psychoanalytic view of personality, which he saw as ensnared by a misplaced biologism, and concluded that even the great Sigmund Freud managed to miss the existence, not to mention the significance, of the human spirit.

How should the psychotherapist address matters of the spirit within the therapeutic process? What exactly has the human spirit to do with what goes on in the therapist's office? As we noted in the last chapter, *pneuma* (spirit) in the New Testament seems to carry with it both an affective and a relational connotation. *Pneuma* is what allows people to maintain interpersonal relationships, and the "quickening of our spirits" by God is what enables us to relate to him as beloved children. These relational capacities are grounded in our ability to feel—to develop those emotional reactions and attachments that seem to characterize the essence of human personhood. Spirit, however, has to do with more than emotions. It also involves intellect, will, and states of consciousness. It has to do with our very mode of being, with our way of positioning ourselves in relation to God, other people, and the universe. Spirit makes possible a quality of life that I will call the mystical.

In this chapter we will take up the difficult subject of mysticism and the mystical, a subject that the Christian church cannot afford to ignore. Moreover, the mystical in one way or another intrudes itself constantly into the psychotherapy process. Mystical concerns and happenings—matters of the spirit—simply cannot be avoided. They emerge regardless of whether or not the therapist or the patient recognizes them for what they are.

Mysticism. Mysticism, which must not be confused with an openness to spiritual mysteries, has thrived for thousands of years in the East. China, India, and Japan, for example, have long been spawning grounds for mystics and mystic cults. The new twist is that large numbers of English-speaking people are now embracing various forms of mysticism as alternatives to "traditional" religion.

Mysticism is not a monolithic thing and it is not easy, therefore, to define it. As I will understand the word, mysticism refers to an altered state of consciousness through which is believed to occur a direct, unmediated union with ultimate reality. This altered state of consciousness is achieved by specific procedures that often involve specialized and well-practiced meditation techniques.

The ultimate reality with which one is said to merge may but does not have to be conceived as "god," either in the sense of an impersonal entity, force, or principle, or in the sense of a transcendent personal God. Ordinarily, the highest mystical attainment is said to involve the loss of any subject-object distinction in conjunction with this "ultimate." The desired oneness is achieved by autonomous human action. There is typically no insistence that mystical experiences unfold at the discretion of a divine sovereign.

Before proceeding, I would like to consider what has been called Christian mysticism. As I suggested above, it is crucial to distinguish between an openness to the presence of mystery and *mysticism*. Through much of the Johannine literature, for example, there are ideas with strong mystical overtones, but these are not mysticistic. Rather, they are signposts pointing to the mysterious ways of the Creator-Provider.

Opening oneself to the mystical may mean to apprehend an ontological mystery, such as the God-man nature of Jesus Christ; to attain knowledge that does not rest on ordinary sense data, such as the existence of eternal life; or to yield to something beyond oneself that is real yet unfathomable, such as the leading of the Holy Spirit. None of this, individually or collectively, amounts to mysticism, for there is no suggestion of becoming part of God or of being able, through human actions alone, to get to God. As Jesus is recorded to have said to Nicodemus (John 3), the Spirit of God neither follows ordinary rules of prediction nor yields to independent human control. Strictly speaking, then, there may be no true Christian mysticism.

It does seem that some extreme forms of pietism come very close to mysticism, which is perhaps the plane along which they are faulted. A related point is that any system of spiritual formation which centers on religious exercises should be used carefully,[2] since it

carries with it the potential for mysticistic abuse.
Nonetheless, I doubt that even these can be called
mysticism. As I will argue shortly, the church seems to
have lost most of its rightful commerce with the
mystical, and many young people discovering this have
turned to the East. It is interesting that this is the part
of the globe from which Christianity itself sprang.
Christianity is, in a quite fundamental sense, an Eastern
religion. In fact, it is more "Eastern"—in the sense in
which I am using this term—than *any* of its rivals.

Physiology and the Mystical. Turning to the physiological,
consider some of the recent advances in brain research.
Ever since Sperry at the California Institute of Technology started to sever the corpus callosum which
connects the two halves of the brain, scientists have
been interested in what, at first, they only guessed to be
two different kinds of mental functioning. It turns out
that the left side of the brain, which basically controls
the right side of the body, is primarily concerned with
verbal logic and sequential reasoning. The right side of
the brain, which controls the left side of the body and
which in most of us is subordinate to the left side of the
brain, is mostly concerned with spatial relations,
aesthetics, patterns, and what is usually called intuition.

To demonstrate how the two cerebral hemispheres
function, a person with a severed corpus callosum
blindly picking up a key right-handedly might be able to
name it but might not be able to select the key, by feel,
from a set of different objects. Alternatively, feeling the
key with the left hand would enable the person to select
it later, by feel, from a collection of objects. But he or
she would not be able to name it. Several physiological
psychologists have suggested that Westerners are
one-sided, captives to left hemisphere thinking.[3]

If this is true, and I believe it is, there may be much
virtue to cultivating the intuitive, holistic, and artistic
styles of mental functioning that seem to characterize
the East, but without adopting the religious
paraphernalia that often comes with this.[4] To some

Christians such a suggestion would seem naive and dangerous, largely because of what they take to be its political implications. It is true that, over the course of history, the percentage of human beings who have been fortunate enough to live under democratic governments is frightfully small, probably less than one-tenth of one percent.[5] Nevertheless, to reject the riches of the East simply because we are leery of a collection of regimes that now rule some of its countries is unreasonable. Recall that the wisdom of the East, as it has been called, goes back several millennia.[6] Communism, as we know it, is less than a century old, and it is of Western origin.

An Irrational Bias Against the Nonrational. It is not unusual to run into even well-educated people who immediately close their ears to anything with an Eastern ring. Yoga, Zen, and meditation are all lumped together and prejudicially dismissed. Not too long ago, for example, I heard a young Christian man from Berkeley speak on the evils that he felt lurked within the breast of Maharishi Mahesh Yogi, the guru of transcendental meditation (TM). He warned that transcendental meditators were poisoning the minds of Americans and that the Students International Meditation Society, or whatever it's called these days, was threatening to take over the government.

That certain meditation "masters" have a knack for business, that at least one has a world plan to make meditation available to everyone on earth, and that meditation has been taught in a few public schools cannot be denied.[7] Neither can the fact that meditation does take on the quality of a religion for many of its practitioners. Meditation surely fills a spiritual void in many people's lives that ought to be filled by Christ. The secret "mantrum" given to TM trainees, for instance, seems to take on for some of them a religious quality.[8]

To jump from this, however, to the conclusion that the procedures of meditation are necessarily a form of spiritualism, or that the words are satanic because they are incomprehensible, is to jump wildly. The forces of evil could most assuredly use meditation to hurt people, but the psychotherapeutic couch—or even the pulpit—would do just as well. Insofar as some people spend time meditating that could better be used for deep prayer, it does them no service, and meditation *may* in some cases become a tragic substitute for faith in God through Christ. This does not mean, however, that there is nothing for us in meditation.

Some years ago I taught a course in altered states of awareness for a local college. My students and I visited several interesting places, including a meditation center, a biofeedback laboratory, a Self-Realization Fellowship temple, a Hindu society meeting place, and a theater which showed samurai movies. We also heard a talk by a Tibetan lama and saw a movie on Tantric chanting. Through the course, it became clear that alien religious practices often go hand-in-hand with techniques to modify states of consciousness. The question is whether one can use the latter without embracing the former and, if so, whether one ought to do so.

The Healthy Expansion of Spiritual Consciousness. Like many other Americans today, I am keenly interested in the East, and the course gave me the chance to pull together my understandings of such diverse enterprises as Zen Buddhism, Hatha Yoga, Sufism, and partial voluntary control of the autonomic nervous system.[9] It also prompted me to reflect further on the nature of prayer and on the meditative use of Scripture. Given that Christianity is said to alter one's internal states, it seems both reasonable and important to explore the relationship between Christian practices, such as prayer and Scripture reading, and the Eastern techniques and arts. To what extent are their effects similar?

On the basis of the scientific literature, it appears that the primary function of activities like chanting or counting breaths may be to focus one's attention so that ordinary thinking processes quiet down.[10] The analogy of lowering the volume on a radio, of screening out left hemisphere chatter, is especially apt for capturing what it is that, say, a TM mantrum may do for the person using it. Since the Eastern disciplines are more existential than analytic, there is some validity to the assertion that they are incapable of adequate verbal description. Still, modulating down associative thinking may be what unifies these diverse disciplines. It is held by meditational adepts, for example, that to ask the meaning of sounds such as the familiar "Om" is a foolish question. The tones are uttered simply for their effects.

Turning to Christianity, it seems undeniable that many Christians are not at peace.[11] We live in a frenetic world and its effects show themselves in our states of mind. The fault is not God's, of course, for it is we who have lost the art of mystical consciousness. The ability to prayerfully withdraw, after the model of Jesus, has all but escaped us. So rooted are we in what sociologist Max Weber called the Protestant work ethic that we are terrified of anything that looks remotely like laziness. We simply do not know *how* to turn down our mental radio volumes, to disengage our cortical computers by resting in the Spirit. If the church is to regain what has been called its lost audience, we may have to offer people much more than the teaching of doctrine. We may need the recrudescence of a *healthy* pietism. Christianity is of the whole person, the right cerebral hemisphere and the limbic system included.[12]

An adequate view of personality has to account for the mystical and a complete psychotherapy must address it. Psychotherapists have often talked about helping people become "centered"—as the great neo-Freudian Karen Horney put it—to live with their centers of gravity inside, instead of outside, of themselves. Perhaps without knowing it, these practitioners were speaking directly or indirectly about a "way of being" that is closely akin to what we are considering here. While I suppose it is entirely possible to be "centered" temporarily and still resist the Holy Spirit, it may be difficult or impossible to embrace God unless one is at least reasonably centered in himself or herself in relation to God.

When we take up the question of how the mystical is to be recovered, in therapy or out of it, we run into something of a theological *cul de sac*. To train ourselves to be potentially more sensitive to things of the Spirit, say by learning to engage the right sides of our brains, seems desirable.[13, 14] However, the development of a true piety, contingent as this is on the sovereign will of God, is not likely to be brought about by merely changing the way we think. Augmented capacities for the mystical may have to be complemented by mature theological guidance and by the moving of God's Spirit. The Christian therapist may not be able to guarantee the operation of the Holy Spirit, but the therapist may at least be able to help the person to become more spiritually aware.

Regardless of the spiritual benefits that may or may not derive from increased "right brain" functioning, there remains the question of the extent to which such functioning helps us physiologically. Does it lower blood pressure, induce relaxation, and facilitate restful sleep? These are empirical questions, to be answered by well-conducted research studies. Although there are a few negative reviews in the literature, it appears that the procedures we have considered have value in helping people bring their physiological processes under better regulation.[15] Parenthetically, it is ethnocentric to argue that biofeedback works because it uses technical instrumentation but that the methods of the East do not. Such a view is more an expression of geographical provincialism than of good scientific judgment.

I have suggested that the Christian church needs to foster the mystical without falling into the quagmires of mysticism. The problem in getting very involved with meditation techniques is that they may become a substitute for a solid devotional life, or for prayer in particular.

Many Christians seem to regard praying as mere verbal recitation. That petitionary prayer is usually verbal cannot be denied, but a rich prayer life consists of more than petitions. On the deepest level, is not the function of prayer to bring us into the mind of Christ?[16] Do not the groanings of the Spirit, alluded to in Romans 8:26, characterize the serious Christian pilgrim? Is it not possible that there may be a psychological parallel between the use of a mantrum and the use of the kinds of foreign words cited in 1 Corinthians 14:4?[17] Might God not intend that, when we pray, we enter into an altered state of consciousness? Perhaps it is meditative prayer that ought to narrow down the Christian's focus of attention so that the frequency and intensity of random associations drop off. To immerse oneself in God,[18] to give him a turn in the meditative dialogue, may be pivotal to deep spirituality. Can we allow ourselves to believe that the Holy Spirit *is* more than a metaphor?

Just as we have a narrow view of prayer, we also sometimes see the Bible myopically, regarding it simply as a compendium of doctrine that gives conceptual answers to religious questions. Perhaps we need to recognize that the modes of consciousness embodied in Scripture are as alien to our natural minds as quantum physics. Scripture refers repeatedly to a qualitative difference between us and God, between our ways and his ways, our thoughts and his thoughts. The New Testament teaches that we need to be transformed by God, through Christ, before we can fully comprehend the things of the Spirit, and that even after regeneration we continue to be caught in a struggle between the Spirit and the flesh. The modes of consciousness of the "natural" person are often just not those of the "spiritual" person. It is as if our minds were tuned to the wrong set of frequencies and we need continual communion with God to keep them spiritually adjusted.[19] To put the matter psychologically, we have the wrong ideas in our minds and the wrong dispositions in our bodies.

For these reasons, memorizing Scripture in a meditative way can be very helpful to one's spiritual walk. It seems to help us know the mind of God. The best way to memorize Scripture is not to race the clock, however, since rushing only ensures left brain dominance. Although trying for quick memorization helps fix the words of the passage in mind, such compulsivity tends to destroy worship and awareness. The best method I have found is, first, to read the Scripture slowly for the flow of the ideas. A few more times through yields a mental outline of the passage. Trying then to repeat it from memory leaves you either stumbling to remember, or aware that you have made additions and omissions, some of which represent substantive changes. It is amazing to see how much one does not grasp in a Scripture paragraph until its meaning is internalized, as if we distort what we memorize so that it matches our mistaken ideas. In psychologist Jean Piaget's terms, we *assimilate* it to our existing cognitive schemata. What we desire, of course, is the accommodation of our schemata to the Way. Through such practice, one can achieve something like the relaxed wakefulness attained through meditation. A similar state of consciousness sometimes occurs in a psychotherapy client when the therapist, at just the right moment, cites a well chosen phrase from Scripture or paraphrases a relevant biblical story.

We should remind ourselves that, while the focus of attention in mysticism seems generally to be on one's own psychological processes, the focus of Christian meditation is ultimately on God. Pressed to the wall, one would have to admit that God reaches us *through* psychological processes such as awareness.[20] Yet, in a living Christianity that makes proper room for mystery, the pivotal consideration is not oneself but a transcendent "personal" intelligence beyond oneself. There is an egocentric tone to many self-help meditation programs. We need to learn what we can from these programs, but it is vitally important to remember that inner psychological workings should not be the Christian's primary concern. It is necessary for us to affirm with the Apostle Paul, "For me to live is Christ."

In this chapter and the last, we surveyed what the New Testament has to say about human personality. We noted that Scripture does not portray itself as a scientific atlas of human behavior, and we found it necessary to look elsewhere for detailed descriptions and predictions of what we are and of what we do. We also noted that secular theories of personality are often infused with significant philosophical or theological ideas that, by definition, are not "scientific." It is therefore necessary to weigh these ideas against the normative material in Scripture, specifically the Pauline anthropology, since it gives us the most complete treatment of the nature of man/woman in the Bible. We took account of the mystical aspect of personality, asking if the church has not neglected it and, thereby, fostered some of the defections to Eastern religions we now see. Christ, we believe, desires the health of the whole person, and therefore we cannot afford to neglect so vital a quality of personality as "spirit." This, I suggest, implies that we must not neglect the affective and intuitive processes by which people seem to apprehend Christian mysteries. Christianity is not a "head trip." It involves wonderfully special states of consciousness to which the Christian therapist must pay attention if psychotherapy is to be what it could and should be.

We will now consider specific forms of contemporary psychotherapy, noting some of their clinical strengths and weaknesses. I will also comment on their theological trappings. To what extent does each take seriously the omnipresence of spirit in human life?

NOTES

1. A helpful, though flawed, article on mysticism by C. G. Thorne, Jr., appears in *The New International Dictionary of the Christian Church*, ed. by J. D. Douglas (Grand Rapids: Zondervan, 1974), pp. 691, 692. The best single volume on the subject is probably *Understanding Mysticism*, ed. by Richard Woods (Garden City: Doubleday, 1980).
2. I am thinking here of Ignatius Loyola's *Spiritual Exercises*.
3. See Robert E. Ornstein, *The Psychology of Consciousness* (San Francisco: Freeman, 1972).
4. Interestingly, some psychotherapists, for example, Otto Rank, put forth the artist as the epitome of mental well-being. See Clara Thompson, *Psychoanalysis: Evolution and Development* (New York: Grove Press, 1959), pp. 174-182.
5. Trust, rather than popular sovereignty or the safeguarding of natural rights, is the common thread running through all forms of democracy. See chapter XVI, "Democracy," in Volume I, *The*

Great Ideas: A Syntopicon of Great Books of the Western World
(Chicago: Encyclopedia Britannica, 1952).

6. See *The Wisdom of China and India*, ed. by Lin Yutang (New York: Random House, 1942).

7. See Harold H. Bloomfield, Michael Peter Cain, and Dennis T. Jaffe, *Transcendental Meditation: Discovering Inner Energy and Overcoming Stress* (New York: Delacorte Press, 1975), pp. 220-228.

8. The mantrum is a beautiful example of a conditional stimulus (CS), since it is used *only* to induce the meditative state. Claims to the contrary, any "meaningless" term such as "rugby don" would probably work.

9. For the first definitive statement on this, see Neal E. Miller, "Learning Visceral and Glandular Responses," *Science*, CLXIII, pp. 434-445.

10. See Ornstein, *The Psychology of Consciousness.*

11. Contrast the themes of rest in the writings of the Chinese Christian martyr Watchman Nee. See his *Sit, Walk, Stand* (Fort Washington, Penn.: Christian Literature Crusade, 1957).

12. A collection of brain centers (cingulate gyrus, hippocampus, amygdala, and septum, all of which are wired into the hypothalamus) of major importance in the generation of emotion.

13. I am *not* saying that such training will necessarily ensure greater spiritual sensitivity, only that it might.

14. See Paul Reps, *Square Sun, Square Moon: A Collection of Sour Sweet Essays* (Rutland, Vt.: Charles E. Tuttel, 1967). Also see *Zen Buddhism: Selected Writings of D. T. Suzuki*, ed. by William Barrett (Garden City: Doubleday, 1956), the best popular introduction to Zen thought and practice.

15. For a set of fascinating articles, see the *Scientific American* reader, *Altered States of Awareness*, ed. by Timothy J. Tyler (San Francisco: Freeman, 1972).

16. I think here of Ephesians 4:15, "growing into Christ," and secondarily of 1 Corinthians 2:16.

17. This text may not refer to prayer.

18. No pantheism is intended here.

19. As I read this over, it seems I am implicitly arguing that, since Easterners are more right hemispheric, they are also *ipso facto* more spiritually receptive. Perhaps they are, which might account for some Eastern phenomena that appear to be truly devilish. On the other hand, an Easterner's possible neglect of the left hemisphere, which I argued is the organ of doctrine, may cancel out the beneficial effects of cultivating the right hemisphere. Good linear logic may be necessary to structure the intuitive movement of nonlinear thought. Appreciation is expressed to Dr. Warren Brown of UCLA for his helpful thoughts on the left-right brain distinction.

20. This touches on the issue of how knowledge relates to awareness. To argue that one can "know" Christ without awareness of Christ is, I suggest, a *non sequitur.*

NINE
CHRISTIANITY AND PSYCHO-THERAPEUTIC METHODS: I

Examining personality theories in the light of Christian theology is no new enterprise, nor is the evaluation of Christianity by secular psychologists.[1, 2] This mutual scrutiny is desirable. It tends to keep participants on both sides of the religious debate honest, and it facilitates healthy intellectual exchange. Persons standing outside of the Christian faith may, through such examination, find that there was something extraordinary about the Galilean nomad after all, while believers, for their part, are reminded that the partition between the church and the world is not a fortress wall but a thin gossamer veil, passage through which, however, is an event of ultimate significance.[3]

It is easy to be lulled into beliefs, professional and otherwise, that are appealing in the moment but which turn out, in the end, to be unsound. Since, as I have suggested, psychotherapists cannot avoid becoming existential guides for their patients, they have a responsibility to weigh the merits of the guidance they provide. Christian therapists need to be especially aware. They stand as Christ's representatives to clients who often engage their services precisely because they *are* Christians. If, as my doctoral student Joseph Hammock insists, every moment is of eternal significance, what goes on between therapist and patient may, indeed, be of monumental importance. Therapists who lumber along in theological and philosophical naiveté may be in cosmic default against those they want to assist.

In this chapter and the next we will survey a number of clinical methods now in common use. As we noted in previous chapters, personality theories and clinical procedures often walk hand-in-hand. Specific beliefs about the nature of human personality are snappy springboards for the invention of "treatment" techniques. Since it is these techniques rather than the theories behind them that the reader is likely to use or have used on him or her, I will focus our attention on identifiable forms of psychotherapy and, where it is appropriate, on the theoretical baggage, moral and metaphysical, that usually comes with them.

It is often the meaning (sometimes arbitrarily) attached to a particular method that makes it from a Christian point of view good or bad. Clinical pragmatism —"if the method works, use it"—usually makes sense in the abstract, provided of course that one's goals are noble. In concrete reality, it turns out to be difficult to use a method without at least implicitly endorsing its philosophical roots. Sometimes this happens because Christian therapists have not thought things through enough to be able to separate theory from practice. Often the procedure is right, insofar as it works, but the ideas surrounding it are not. In such instances, Christian therapists need the flexibility to use procedures without knowing exactly why they are effective. Naturally, I am assuming that these procedures are not intrinsically offensive to the Christian conscience.

How is the Christian therapist to know which ideas are sound and which are not? If the idea is philo-sophical-theological in nature, and if it manifestly flies in the face of Christian belief as this has developed over the course of twenty centuries, there is a very good chance that the idea is quite simply wrong. No doubt the church can be wrong. No doubt a practitioner can be correct where many theologians have not been. In my judgment, however, the weight of probability for right opinion is heavily on the side of theological tradition. This suggests that Christian therapists ought to be cautious in the face of the temptation to "straighten out" Christian theology. As I have argued throughout this book, it is better to live with tension than to resolve it capriciously and unworthily.

We will consider: behavior therapy; client-centered counseling; biofeedback; hypnosis; transactional analysis; family therapy and marriage counseling; existential analysis; interpersonal psychotherapy; sensitivity and encounter groups; cognitive behavior modification; Gestalt therapy; various body-oriented approaches; and, of course, psychoanalysis. There are, to be sure, many other kinds of psychotherapy, for example Jungian analysis and Adlerian therapy, but I have chosen to evaluate only those types in widest use.

Every legitimate form of psychotherapy probably has something of value in it. This is because human beings are incredibly complex and multifaceted. Most of us would probably do well to: learn new behaviors (behavior therapy); experience love and acceptance from an authentic person and thereby become more emotionally free (client-centered counseling); bring some of our physiological processes under better control (biofeedback); absorb constructive "suggestions" deep into our minds (hypnosis); play fewer destructive games and enact a more effective life script (transactional analysis); resolve family struggles more effectively (family or marriage therapy); explore the meaning of life more deeply and fully (existential therapy); become more intimate with other people (interpersonal therapy); find out from them how we come across (various group therapies); say more benevolent and sensible things to ourselves (rational-emotive therapy); make contact with the disowned parts of us (Gestalt therapy); have our bodies realigned and our tensions released (body-oriented therapies); and, gain further insight into our intrapsychic workings (psychoanalysis). This list could go on and on.

Many times the question is not "What will help?" but "What will most effectively and efficiently help?" Which method, administered by which therapist, is most suitable for *this* problem in *this* person? Certain therapists, sometimes from foolishness and sometimes from vanity, proffer the way they "do therapy" as if it were the perfect choice for every client. They seem like Old West sideshow barkers selling, for a dollar a bottle, "The Elixir of Earth." Whatever ails you, the Elixir is touted as the treatment of choice.

Before we begin our survey, I should emphasize that what I will offer are my opinions and judgments, based not on research studies for the most part but rather on my experience as a practitioner and teacher of psychotherapy. As a matter of fact, for most of the issues we will address there are no definitive research studies. Among the disappointments of behavioral science is the realization that even after years of intensive research we are still very much in the dark about the actual process of therapy.[4] We know that therapy "works" —although researchers debate whether it works any better than such everyday remedies as talks with one's barber-beautician—but studies intended to find out which kinds of therapy are "best" have generally failed. The "active ingredients" of human helping procedures are still very much at issue. With this *caveat*, let us begin.

BEHAVIOR THERAPY

Few methods of therapy have received as much publicity during the past decade as those based, more or less, on conditioning procedures. I say "more or less" because, as perceptive critics like Paul Wachtel have pointed out, many behavior therapy techniques are at best loosely derived from the theoretical roots by which they are rationalized.[5]

Conditioning is often said to be "the simplest form of learning." The belief undergirding behavior therapy is that nearly all human learning is, at base, conditioning. Learning in this context is not intended to mean just the memorization of facts or the acquisition of a skill but *any* relatively permanent modification of behavior that results from practice or experience.

There are two fundamental types of conditioning: classical (also known as Type I or respondent conditioning) and instrumental (also known as Type II or operant conditioning). Classical conditioning is typically said to explain the learning of involuntary (autonomic) behavior, for example getting nervous before exams. Instrumental conditioning is typically said to explain the learning of voluntary behavior, for example, asserting one's views in an argument. We should note that some theorists endeavor to explain autonomic behavior (Type I) in operant (Type II) terms, while others try to explain voluntary (Type II) behavior in respondent (Type I) terms; in other words, some researchers believe that there is only one kind of conditioning—*which* kind is a matter of opinion. This is neither here nor there for the purposes of our discussion.

Behavior therapies are appealing because of their apparent simplicity, and also because they work eminently well for certain kinds of problems. To demonstrate these points, I will briefly consider two popular forms of behavior therapy, one based on classical conditioning and the other based on operant conditioning.

Desensitization is a technique for reducing fear.[6] Although there are many ways to do desensitization, the customary way is to get the client to relax while having him or her imagine successively closer encounters with feared events, situations, or activities. In essence, the "dosage" or the "exposure" is gradually increased, while having the patient experience something antithetical to anxiety.[7] A person afraid of flying, for example, might be asked to imagine, first, approaching the airport, and eventually, sitting in the plane as it takes off, gets caught in turbulence, and so on. Unless fears are resistant to treatment because they are psychodynamically complex and serve some hidden purpose (I have had at least two such cases), desensitization is an efficient and effective way to ameliorate most irrational fears. Using it, I have successfully treated fears of: elevators, public speaking, dating, spiders, flying, sex, criticism, test taking, driving, talking on the phone, heights, small closed spaces, talking honestly with loved ones, authority figures, and probably a host of others I cannot recall.

Turning to operant methods, suppose a young man is very shy toward members of the opposite sex and wants help to overcome this (see the case of Robert in chapter 4). One way of proceeding would be to have him keep a daily record of relevant events, for example, the number of conversations he has with "eligibles," the number of these he initiates, by phone or in person, the number of social invitations he issues, etc. Each of these event categories might be given a value, say five for each phone call completed and ten for each social invitation issued. At the end of every week, perhaps during the therapy hour, these points could be redeemed, say for cash or various activities that the young man has reported to be "reinforcing" (e.g., going to the movies). The client might be taught to reinforce himself or herself, perhaps to make rewards contingent on taking social risks. Operant methods such as these have been used effectively to treat a variety of problems, in a wide range of settings, from classrooms to hospitals. They have been found especially effective with children and with the seriously disturbed, such as "backward schizophrenics" who have deteriorated to the point where they no longer care for their own basic physical needs.[8]

There are a number of problems that surround the use of conditioning methods, but before pointing out some of them, I would like to suggest that any powerful influence tool can be used for evil. Thus, commonly heard concerns about "brainwashing," "1984," and so on are more appropriately addressed to people (conditioners) than to the tool (conditioning).

Turning to the problems, there is the ethical problem of coercion. This seems not to be much of a difficulty at the two ends of the freedom spectrum, e.g., with adult outpatients who knowingly request conditioning treatment, and with persons so mentally regressed that almost *any* way to help seems superior to doing nothing. Perhaps the biggest potential ethical problem inheres in treating children, whether the reinforcement is dispensed by the parent, the teacher, or the therapist.

I have written elsewhere of how attempts to control a child by regulating behavioral consequences may tragically backfire.[9] Behavior therapists would counter that we inadvertently reinforce children anyway, so why not do it more beneficially and systematically? There is certainly something to be said for this line of argument. At the same time, as one of B. F. Skinner's students eventually concluded, there may be a crucial difference between "natural" and "arbitrary" reinforcers.[10] In altering one set of contingencies—rules for what behaviors lead to what outcomes—we may inadvertently change others.

For example, letting Johnny stay up an extra hour in return for not hitting Junior may, indeed, reduce the frequency of his violent assaults. It may at the same stroke, however, increase the frequency of Johnny's father's assaults on everyone, since Father may quickly come to resent the new intrusion into *his* time alone with Mother. Moreover, Father is not likely to tell this to the therapist. He would be too embarrassed and, more basically, he may not even realize *why* he finds himself less patient with the family. This relationship between the new program for Johnny and the increase in her husband's irritability may also escape the mother's notice, as she is likely to find herself befuddled and depressed by the whole thing. These sorts of relationships among various behavioral contingencies are the rule rather than the exception, especially in outpatient family work, and it may be myopic to assume that we can always anticipate and defuse them.

A second problem with conditioning methods has been well articulated by David Brokaw, a student of mine.[11] Through an excellent literature review, he has shown that behavior therapists have tended to be simplistic in assuming, contrary to their own dicta, that reinforcers can routinely be specified in advance. Praise from Mother may *not* be a reward but rather a punishment for a particular child, especially if the child perceives her as malevolent and manipulative. It is the meaning, the perception, of the "consequence" that counts. Wise behavior therapists know this, but not all behavior therapists are wise.

These criticisms apply most pointedly to operant practitioners, but they are relevant to proponents of classical conditioning techniques as well. For example, patients may be persuaded to undergo desensitization for things that the therapist misguidedly believes they should "be comfortable with and not avoid" (e.g., casual sex). It is also possible to modify the patient's response to one "stimulus" without taking into account its wider context (e.g., fear of walking over a high bridge, this in a person with strong but unexpressed suicidal wishes). And interventions may be ineffective. The criticisms I have mentioned are *not* unique to behavior therapy, and they have no unique theological importance that I can see. The next problem does.

All but the most theoretically urbane behavior therapists treat feelings as secondary, sometimes even as unimportant or trivial. The criticism that behavior therapists tend to neglect or disparage the role of emotions in human living is often rebutted, ineffectively in my judgment, by the claim that behavior therapists do value feelings but that they try to alter them by changing behavior. Quite aside from the patient's presenting problem, it is difficult to believe that most behavior therapists ever make anything but behavior their serious concern. As Ortega y Gasset has argued, it is not reason (or language) but emotions that make one a human being.[12] God is no behaviorist.

Having to this point purposely avoided the word behaviorism, I would now like to define it. "Methodo-logical behaviorism" is nothing more nor less than good behavioral science. It is a research method having to do with how concepts are defined ("operationally"). As such, it has nothing whatever to do with "philosophical behaviorism," the behaviorism of Skinner and the popular press. Philosophical behaviorists—and not all behavior therapists belong in this category—devalue mental processes and anything else that cannot be seen and touched (e.g., love, joy, peace, and altruistic sentiments). In general, they want to *reduce* the unseen, either to the material or to the epiphenomenal. A careful reading of Skinner's *Beyond Freedom and Dignity* will reveal this.[13]

I have written a more extended discussion of these issues elsewhere.[14] While methodological behaviorism is to be valued for its scientific merits, and behavior therapy is to be esteemed for its clinical power, philosophical behaviorism is incompatible with a good deal of Christian doctrine. We have given behavior therapy, and behaviorism, more space than we shall give to most of the other methods in our discussion because it is absolutely vital that Christians know about both, and about the difference(s) between them.

ROGERIAN THERAPY

Client-centered counseling (also known as Rogerian therapy) is almost the antithesis of behavior therapy. The concern of the Rogerian is not with overt behavior but with feelings.[15] A client-centered therapist is, first and foremost, interested in how the client perceives and affectively responds to the world. People consult therapists primarily for disorders of behavior or for disorders of consciousness. The behavior therapist is clearly geared up for treating the former, while the client-centered counselor is obviously oriented toward treating the latter.

Carl Rogers developed the "nondirective" approach to therapy, working initially with college students, and it has become more and more the backbone of clinical and counseling training in United States universities. Only behavioral methods give it competition.

Rogerian help is called nondirective because the client-centered therapist assumes that the client—not "patient"—knows himself or herself best and is, therefore, the ultimate judge of what to talk about in therapy and how to make everyday life decisions. The key idea informing this therapy is that, under proper therapeutic conditions, people will invariably grow, since all of us have an innate drive to become "fully functioning persons."

What exactly constitutes the proper therapeutic atmosphere? One characterized by unconditional positive regard (nonpossessive warmth), genuineness (congruence), and accurate empathy on the part of the therapist. Instead of dealing in behavioral prescriptions, as does the behavior therapist, or in interpretations of intrapsychic dynamics, as does the psychoanalyst (see next chapter), the client-centered counselor provides "reflections." These are statements that capture the emotional essence of what the client communicates and which tend to move the client a little deeper into feelings. Through being understood by a warm and sincere therapist who renders no evaluative judgment, the client grows in awareness, attends more to the "wisdom of the organism," and allows previously unacknowledged feelings to emerge.

It is probably of significance that Carl Rogers was raised in what he describes as a Christian home. No other theory of therapy sounds quite so much like the skillful administration of grace—not easy-to-roll-off-the-tongue grace, but deeply meaningful interpersonal acceptance and communion. The good Rogerian therapist is much like the epitome of a wise and patient friend. He or she may be the most concrete and personal encounter with godlikeness that many people will ever have. A great deal of healing has been facilitated by able Rogerians.

I have three concerns about client-centered therapy. First, like behavior therapists but in the opposite direction, Rogerians may be a little one-sided. What people actually *do* matters, both of itself and in how it indirectly affects feelings (e.g., Harry acts nasty to other people, which leads them to reject him, which prompts him to act nasty, and so on, in repeating circles).

Second, precisely because Rogerian therapy can be so grace-filled, Christian Rogerians have a special responsibility to identify themselves as believers. God, in other words, should be given the credit as the ultimate source of all grace. For a Rogerian who works in a setting where virtually all clients are Christian and know that the therapist is too, the problem essentially vanishes, but for a Rogerian in a secular setting it surely remains.

Finally, Rogers seems to have thrown off his religious heritage in large measure, retaining the form but not the substance of Christianity. While it is probably true that most people want to grow, there is also the matter of human perversity (Adolf Hitler accomplished his atrocities less than half a century ago). The "radical nature of evil" must be reckoned with, confronted for what it is, and no amount of wishful thinking will change this. Neither will a renewal of belief in Rousseau's "noble savage." Like it or not, people have to come to grips with their own frailty—their own sinfulness—although I am quite ready to agree that it is ordinarily not the therapist's job to point that out! Perhaps people are *most* likely to do this within the Rogerian climate of nurturing. By the same token, it seems contrary to the best interests of the client to express, or imply, that evil is innocuous, effete, and generally to be dealt with by a wave of the finger and a genteel "tsk . . . tsk." While most Christian Rogerians recognize and deal honestly with this potential difficulty in their therapy, all do not. There is the risk that their patients will throw off the rigor of Christianity for a religion of feeling, a religion that amounts to what, as we saw earlier, Paul Vitz terms "selfism."[16] Let us now consider a therapeutic approach that departs substantially from the Rogerian's concern with subjectivity and client-centered emotional exploration.

BIOFEEDBACK

Biofeedback has much in common with behavior therapy, in that it has to do with if-then relationships, with contingencies. As the name biofeedback implies, the basic paradigm is to provide people with information about one or more of their physiological processes—e.g., heart rate, blood pressure, patterns of electrical brain activity (EEGs), muscle tension—in order to help them learn how to bring these processes under more voluntary control.[17] It takes little expertise to see the potential value of this. Disorders like hypertension (high blood pressure) kill people, and biofeedback is therefore potentially life-saving.

Because both biofeedback and behavior therapy directly concern behavior and only secondarily have to do with psychological states, I am not sure that either one is, strictly speaking, a psychotherapy. Yet, both have obvious psychotherapeutic effects. Happily, biofeedback does not have strong ties with behaviorist rhetoric and, therefore, it is far less philosophically troublesome.

There can be little theological objection to a set of methods intended to bring the body under better conscious regulation, unless of course one wants to take a stance against all applications of technology in the vicinity of the human psyche. Some thinkers do take such a position, arguing that behavioral techniques of any kind only serve to buttress a "mechanomorphic" view of the person. Frankly, I feel this is going too far.

The major problem with biofeedback may be in its overselling. Such overselling is easy to do—patients often do it themselves—because of all the scientific gadgets used. Biofeedback is of demonstrably more value for disorders of a psychophysiological nature than for those in which the role of the body is more ambiguous. Biofeedback is highly unlikely to cure chronic depression or to alter deeply ingrained paranoid beliefs—though it certainly may cure excess tension in an executive.

The great virtue of biofeedback lies in its capacity to provide direct access to the physical correlates of psychological states. Psychotherapists, including some psychiatric physicians who should know better, have generally neglected the body, especially as it interacts with the mind. Biofeedback is changing all this.

HYPNOSIS

Hypnosis, like biofeedback, can be used to bring certain physical phenomena under mental control. Altering the temperature of the subject's hands and changing sensitivity to pain are common examples. Hypnosis is usually used clinically, however, not for the regulation of autonomic physiological processes but for the alteration of troubling habits, such as smoking, overeating, or making self-defeating statements to oneself.

Although researchers have long debated the nature of hypnosis,[18] no one quite knows what it is. At least, no single view has received universal acceptance among investigators. Is the hypnotic state a special mode of consciousness, or is it simply a sophisticated form of roleplaying? It seems to me to be a highly focused state of awareness, such that ordinary vigilance is suspended, and control for one's safety is turned over temporarily to an authority figure. But this is merely an undocumented opinion.

Because of all the theatrical associations that come to mind when one thinks of hypnotism, it is easy to overlook the fact that hypnosis has a noble clinical heritage. During the middle of the nineteenth century, entire hospitals were established in India for the purpose of performing surgery on patients under hypnosis (the British were too conservative to allow this at home). Recall that, prior to this time, there were no effective and safe anesthetics. All surgeries, including amputations, were done while the poor patient was conscious. Had it not been for the discovery of chloroform, nitrous oxide, and a few other related chemicals in the 1840s, the hypnosis movement might well have progressed further.

It should be noted that people in hypnotic states are not asleep, nor can they usually be induced to do things patently at odds with their basic moral values. For this reason, I see no particular theological problem attending the use of hypnosis, especially since this use is not ordinarily coupled with any philosophical or religious position. And, like biofeedback, it seems to be a potentially useful tool. Two cautionary remarks are, nonetheless, worth making.

First, most patients who come to a therapist requesting hypnosis want a fast and painless cure. Unfortunately, for most psychological troubles there are no quick, and certainly no easy solutions. Psychotherapy, if it is to work, often takes time and frequently requires that the patient go through a fair amount of temporary agony. I am not saying what I wish to be true but, rather, what *is* true.

Second, although I know several competent and respected clinicians who use hypnosis, I am routinely skeptical about hypnotherapists. This is because the practice of hypnosis seems to draw more than its fair share of strange and offbeat people. To feel comfortable about a particular hypnotist, I need to know that he or she is demonstrably well trained and that such use as he or she makes of hypnosis is well thought out.

NOTES

1. See Hans Küng's recent book, *Freud and the Problem of God* (New Haven: Yale University Press, 1979).
2. Erich Fromm, *The Dogma of Christ* (New York: Holt, Rinehart and Winston, 1955) and Jay Haley, *The Power Tactics of Jesus Christ* (New York: Avon, 1969).
3. David A. Hubbard, president of Fuller Theological Seminary, remarked in a sermon given in the Fuller chapel that the division between the church and the world is not a fortress wall but a thin line.
4. Allen E. Bergin and Michael J. Lambert, "The Evaluation of Therapeutic Outcomes," in Sol L. Garfield and Allen E. Bergin's (eds.) *Handbook of Psychotherapy and Behavior Change: An Empirical Analysis*, second ed. (New York: Wiley, 1978).
5. Paul E. Wachtel, *Psychoanalysis and Behavior Therapy: Toward an Integration* (New York: Basic Books, 1977).
6. Marvin R. Goldfried and Gerald C. Davison, *Clinical Behavior Therapy* (New York: Holt, Rinehart and Winston, 1976), especially chapter 6.

7. *Ibid.*

8. See the excellent reference list at the end of Charles Wallace's "Assessment of Psychotic Behavior," in Michael Hersen and Alan S. Bellack's (eds.) *Behavioral Assessment: A Practical Handbook* (New York: Pergamon, 1976).

9. Clinton W. McLemore and Lorna Smith Benjamin, "Whatever Happened to Interpersonal Diagnosis?: A Psychosocial Alternative to DSM-III," *American Psychologist* 34 (1979): 17-34, especially p. 27.

10. Charles Ferster's comments years ago at the Annual Southern California Conference on Behavior Modification.

11. The tentative title of David W. Brokaw's and my article describing this work is, "Toward a More Rigorous Definition of Social Reinforcement."

12. Jose Ortega y Gasset, *What Is Philosophy?* (New York: Norton, 1960).

13. B. F. Skinner, *Beyond Freedom and Dignity* (New York: Alfred A. Knopf, 1971) and *About Behaviorism* (New York: Alfred A. Knopf, 1974).

14. Clinton W. McLemore, "Can a Christian Be a Behaviorist?" *Journal of the American Scientific Affiliation* 30 (1978): 45, 46.

15. In my opinion, the best all-around introduction to Rogerian therapy is Carl R. Rogers' *On Becoming a Person: A Therapist's View of Psychotherapy* (Boston: Houghton Mifflin, 1961).

16. Paul C. Vitz, *Psychology as Religion: The Cult of Self-Worship* (Grand Rapids: Eerdmans, 1977).

17. Barbara Brown, *New Mind, New Body* (New York: Harper & Row, 1974).

18. See, for example, E. Hilgard's *The Experience of Hypnosis* (New York: Harcourt, Brace and World, 1968).

TEN
CHRISTIANITY AND PSYCHO-THERAPEUTIC METHODS: II

In the last chapter, we discussed several forms of psychological help that are widely used, frequently requested, and commonly mentioned in the mass media. These were behavior therapy, Rogerian counseling, biofeedback, and hypnosis.

In this chapter we will continue our survey of psychotherapeutic methods, focusing on transactional analysis, family therapy, marriage counseling, existential analysis, interpersonal therapy, group techniques, cognitive behavior modification, Gestalt therapy, some body-oriented approaches and, finally, the grandparent of all psychotherapies, psychoanalysis. In general we will treat these methods more briefly than we did those in the preceding chapter.

TRANSACTIONAL ANALYSIS

Transactional analysis is primarily a way of bringing to light the "games people play" and the "scripts" by which they live. Games are by nature manipulative—they involve an ulterior motive—and they are sometimes deadly serious.

Let us imagine that Tom, a college student, says to his friend Harry, "That old buzzard Jones is really a rat, isn't he? Giving us all that work to do over vacation." Assume that Harry answers, "Yeah! He sure is. I bet that miserable excuse for an English teacher doesn't have a warm bone in his body." So far, the conversation is straightforward. Tom has criticized Professor Jones and Harry has chimed in.

But suppose that Tom then jumps back in righteous indignation and says, "That's the trouble with you, Harry. You're always so negative about everyone!" Poor Harry has been taken. He thought that Tom invited him to complain about Jones, but when he did he got sandbagged. With good reason, Harry feels as if he has been set up and double-crossed.

This element of unpleasant surprise is characteristic of games. Someone, somewhere along the line, usually gets ambushed. Games also characteristically have a payoff, and in our example perhaps the payoff for Tom is that he can ventilate his critical attitudes on someone else, or even justify his view that others cannot be trusted. After all, didn't Harry judge Jones harshly?

Scripts, in contrast to games, are life patterns. Some people, for example, cannot allow themselves to succeed and will do all sorts of self-sabotaging things to prevent success from overtaking them, regardless of what they may *say* about wanting to do well.

Beyond games and scripts, transactional analysts also talk about "strokes," "trading stamps," and so on. Eric Berne's introduction to "TA," *Games People Play* is still timely and worth reading, and there are a number of other popular introductions to this school of treatment available.[1, 2]

A large part of transactional analysis has to do with revealing the nature of an individual's games and scripts to him or her. This is done via humor, chalkboard diagrams, or whatever else is likely to highlight the "ego states" involved (parent, adult, child) as well as their accompanying crossed transactions. Tom, for instance, communicated to Harry that he wanted to have an adult to adult (or perhaps child to child) conversation, but then Tom "crossed" this transaction with his hidden agenda of criticizing Harry (critical parent to child). Often

TA is done in groups, with one therapist treating several patients simultaneously, who also "treat" each other as well.

For some psychotherapy clients, orthodox TA methods may be a little too "intellectual" a treatment to get at the root of the problem(s). Tom may need to cry out how *he* felt criticized and left in the lurch as a child more than he needs an analysis of his social transactions. I do not want to overstress this, however, since all seasoned therapists seem ultimately to deal with deep feelings. The theoretical structure of TA is clever and in many places innovative.

Theologically, I view TA as an exceedingly valuable contribution, insofar as it brings into sharp relief the complexities of human interpersonal behavior as well as the manipulative subtlety of which we, as human beings, are regrettably capable.

MARRIAGE AND FAMILY THERAPY

Family therapy, of which there are many kinds, is usually aimed at changing the family "system."[3] To the extent that it focuses on what amounts to games between family members and on the family script, it resembles TA. Specific persons within the family are often said to fill roles, for example "conforming child," "parents' assistant," "bad child," "scapegoat," and "peacemaker." Most family therapists try to understand what happens, good and bad, in terms of the family as a self-regulating entity.

It may be discovered, for example, that Dad subtly, even unwittingly, encourages Johnny's misbehavior— misbehavior which Father, of course, condemns. Johnny's misdeeds, in turn, may keep Mom and Dad so wrapped up in crisis that they can avoid facing their marital problems. While the heat is on Johnny, the heat is off them. It may turn out that they cannot talk to each other without an argument, unless they are talking about their son. He gives them something to agree on, that life with Johnny is awful.

Often what is going on within a family is a good deal

less nefarious. In some cases, family members simply need a forum for communication, which therapy regularly provides. It also provides an outside (objective) moderator, facilitator, and model. Through demonstrating *how* to communicate, the therapist helps people in the family communicate with each other. Much of this comes to communication training, the mainstay of which is learning to put feelings into words (e.g., "I feel terrible when you don't answer me").

In the hands of a competent and responsible professional, family treatment can be strikingly effective. Such services are an obvious resource for the church, whose "ministries to families" are often superficial. The potential pitfalls of family therapy are almost all clinical in nature.

Systems of *any* kind are very resilient to change and, in the case of families, there is frequently strong resistance to alteration. As soon as the therapist gets close to the heart of the trouble, one or more family members are quite likely to decide that "things aren't so bad after all," perhaps they "shouldn't have come," etc. It takes a highly skilled therapist to head off such attrition, especially since the point of many family sessions is to air grievances and to resolve conflicts. Since customarily *someone* in the family has a vested interest in maintaining the status quo, not everyone *wants* all grievances aired and conflicts resolved. Family members who like the way resources are currently being allocated within the prevailing "system" try very hard to keep it intact. Whether the resource in question is the family car, vacation money, or just plain time, it *feels* as if someone is going to win and, by implication, someone is going to lose!

The skill of the therapist, in such instances, lies in his or her ability to bring about a solution that gives everyone the sense of gaining, of "making a profit." For family members who control more resources than others, this often involves getting them to trade in one kind of power for another. In return for relinquishing coercive power, the power of force, they gain the power of influence, persuasion, and intimacy—in short, the power of affection.

While we are talking of family interventions, I want to say something about marriage counseling. The difference between the two is that family therapy ordinarily includes children, while marriage counseling obviously focuses on the relationship between husband and wife. Clearly, since children are often a source of considerable stress to a marriage, the lines separating marital and family therapy are sometimes fuzzy. Most of what I have said about family therapy could be said of marriage counseling.

It should be noted that in many states there is no regulation whatever over who can "practice" as a marriage counselor. Just about anyone can hold himself or herself out to the public as a marriage specialist in most parts of the country. As a consequence, many marriage counselors have few credentials and are ill-trained. Some are simply quacks.

In terms of the actual conduct of marital treatment, it has been well documented that when there is significant marital trouble and professional help is sought, both spouses should be involved in the remedial process.[4] I would guess that no small number of divorces have been helped along by a well-meaning therapist working with only one spouse. The unilateral treatment of what is, by nature, a two-person entity is likely to turn out to be just that, unilateral—one-sided. Such treatment is easily capable of further alienating the uninvolved person.

Regarding separations, I believe them much more likely to hurt than to help an ailing marriage. It has been said that marriage is the hardest job in the world. Even at its best, it can certainly be among the most demanding of relationships, which is why it is the rare marriage that has been entirely devoid of trouble. To a person who has been experiencing years of marital strife, any kind of separation is going to feel as refreshing as water to a thirsty nomad. It is like sleep to an over-worked doctor. Under the spell of such refreshment, a maritally troubled person is very much at risk—in danger of making decisions (e.g., divorce) for which he or she may later be sorry. (After all, who wants to drink the whole oasis or sleep forever?) Furthermore, separated persons are particularly vulnerable to forming attachments to other people. Since they do not entail the reservoir of resentment that builds up in almost any marriage (fallen creatures that we are!), new relationships offer to augment the refreshment of separation. While these relationships may be very healing, it is by no means certain that they will wear any better over time than the ones they replace. The nomad's thirst is rarely quenched permanently by moving to a nearby country—that also has its deserts—nor is the doctor's fatigue alleviated by joining the staff of another hospital which, alas, also has its stressful and demanding emergency room!

EXISTENTIAL THERAPY

Marriage therapy and family therapy seem very concrete, very immediate. Existential analysis and psychotherapy, however, concern matters more abstract (though perhaps just as immediate). "What gives your life meaning?" "Are you living authentically?" "Do you accept responsibility for your life, for your project of existence?"

These are the kinds of questions that an existential practitioner is likely to put to the patient. They are, of course, not idle questions. They reach to the core of human living, which is possibly why philosophers with emotional sensitivity are occasionally very good therapists. Existentially oriented therapists are openly and expressly concerned with philosophical, and by implication with theological, questions. This stands in refreshing contrast to clinicians who either pretend or mistakenly believe themselves and their treatments to be unrelated to such matters. Only a strict behavior technician could claim such philosophic neutrality, and even this is debatable.

While the honesty of the existential clinician may be welcomed, his or her particular beliefs may not be. We noted above how the Rogerian therapist who does not profess Christ may mislead people into viewing someone or something other than God as the ultimate source of grace. The existentialist who is not a Christian may imbue people, overtly or covertly, knowingly or unknowingly, with a world view that both conflicts with Christianity and serves, in the end, as a religion. No matter how Socratic and nondoctrinaire the existential practitioner, his or her philosophical-theological ideas are going to be communicated to the patient, and the patient—who has now become more attuned to metaphysical and ethical questions—is probably going to listen. Clichés like "existence precedes essence" and others, suggesting that persons must make their own choices and therefore should not look to the therapist for metaphysical and ethical answers, do *not* alter the basic human tendency to do so.[5] Neither do they change the therapist's quite human tendency to suggest them!

These criticisms to the side, however, it must be acknowledged that existential therapists have courageously gone about the business of helping people with their ultimate, and therefore critical, questions. They have dared explicitly to raise issues that nearly always surface some time during therapy, whether implicitly or explicitly. This courage represents a healthy challenge and perhaps a model for the Christian psychotherapist.

INTERPERSONAL THERAPY

Most schools of therapy do not pose abstract philosophic questions to the patient, at least not in so many words. Often, however, the school *is* a school—a collection of like-minded practitioners—precisely because it has decided *what* in life has the power to confer meaning, what it *means* to live according to true human nature, and just who *is* responsible for what. Interpersonal psychotherapy, or "interpersonal psychiatry" as it is sometimes called, is one example.[6]

To the interpersonalist, communication is the very essence of humanness, particularly communication that fosters intimacy. With intimacy comes a decrease in anxiety, and an increase in felt security. While the existential clinician is likely to view anxiety as potentially productive and therefore well worth enduring (e.g., *angst*), the interpersonal therapist sees it as the bane of humankind and the core of psychopathology. Anxiety, at root, comes from experiences with other people.

To paraphrase Harry Stack Sullivan, the father of interpersonal psychiatry, "it takes people to make people sick, and it takes people to make people better." Others, most notably parents, create in us our losses of "euphoria" and, therefore, our anxieties and troubles. The contagion of anxiety results in a flawed ability to sort out experiences and, correspondingly, in a lowered capacity to articulate to others what it is exactly that we think and feel. This, in turn, leads to a deficit in interpersonal closeness that deprives us of both social comfort and routine correction of disordered thinking. The need for such correction is what makes it important, for example, for everyone to have a close friend during childhood. Such a friend usually straightens out, persistently and unobstrusively, our idiosyncratic ideas—about ourselves, our families, and society. "I'm special." "No one else could possibly feel the way I do." "People can't be trusted." "My parents are always right." These are the sorts of notions that ordinarily yield to more realistic conceptions under the informal tutelage of an intimate friend.

The interpersonal therapist serves as a surrogate friend, specifically as an expert in what is, and what is not, an accurate apprehension of social reality. Along the way, he or she also provides the client with practice at intimate communication, since the *sine qua non* of good interpersonal treatment is a close but professional relationship between doctor and patient. Obviously the therapist must be adroit at establishing and sustaining such a relationship, often with a person who in one way or another makes this difficult. If things go well, the progressing client can carry more and more of this burden until the two are eventually relating pretty much as two equal human beings. The therapist has moved, then, from the role of skilled artist to that of knowing peer.

Scripture seems to indicate clearly that human beings, created as reflections of God, are by nature relational. Interpersonal therapy appears, therefore, to fit nicely into a Christian framework. If our relationships with God and with people are inseparably connected (see the first epistle of John in the New Testament), what could be more psychologically beneficial than helping a patient relate better to other people? It is possible that the upper limit of one's capacity to relate to God is ordinarily fixed at the upper limit of one's capacity to relate to other human beings (again see 1 John), which is perhaps why we see so much neurotic religiosity and also why the body of Christ is so important to an individual's faith. We *need* healthy relationships with Christians if we are to survive on this planet as Christians relating to an invisible God. Such relationships are growth-producing. They help us grow as *persons, as children of a heavenly Father.*

The major theological problem I see with interpersonal psychotherapy is that, like most other therapies, it makes no explicit room for God or for the kinds of existential questions we discussed above. Such questions themselves might be viewed as pathological. On the clinical side, interpersonal therapies may at times downplay the roles of both strong feelings and overt behavior change. Still, I regard the interpersonal approach as among the more balanced of the options available in the professional marketplace. Sophisticated interpersonalists are well aware that crucial relationships may be "in the head" (e.g., internal conversations with deceased loved ones) and also that present styles of social behavior (e.g., choosing sadistic associates) may maintain psychological problems (e.g., depression).

GROUPS

Sensitivity and encounter groups might seem to be closely related to interpersonal therapy, and I suppose in some ways they are. Both traditions pay a great deal of attention to human relationships and both involve the giving of information—"feedback"—to a client about *how* he or she relates. The differences, however, are substantial.

Aside from the obvious difference that one occurs in an individual and the other in a group format, there is the fact that sensitivity and encounter groups are not expressly identified as psychotherapy. Indeed, many well-known group leaders make a special point of saying that what they do is *not* for the abnormal but for the normal.

Another difference has to do with the extent to which what goes on in the immediate present is the focus of attention. While the interpersonal therapist pays a good bit of notice to what the client is doing with or to the therapist—with what kinds of interpersonal structures he or she is attempting to create—a lot of attention is also paid to relationships outside the office. These include relationships that ended years ago, for example, with parents during childhood.

Finally, the interpersonal psychotherapist is highly attuned to internal psychodynamics and spends considerable time trying to make sense, say, of what it is about eating in public that makes Mr. Johnson irrationally angry at his mother. Concern with past relationships, relationships with others outside the therapy group, or mental dynamics are not character- istic of sensitivity and encounter groups, which usually focus on what has been called the "here and now."[7]

Despite the horror stories one hears about people who have been devastated by bad group experiences, a well-conducted group of the sort we are discussing can be very helpful. It is not at all uncommon to run into people who are entirely oblivious to their impact on others, or who are grossly inept at expressing how they feel and what they think. Sensitivity groups are oriented more toward the former, while encounter groups are oriented more toward the latter.

Problems with groups stem more from individual leaders than from group methods per se. For reasons not too hard to fathom, group work has drawn more than its share of "facilitators" who act out, via their groups, the game of "let's you and him fight."[8] This reality, however regrettable, does not obviate the value of well-run group experiences.

Concerning group therapy as a sole form of treatment, I have the reservation that what is "now" may not be "here," i.e., what may be of most vital significance to and for a patient may have little to do with the present "group process." We should also note that sensitivity and encounter groups do not come from the same roots. "Sensitivity training" originated over thirty years ago in New England, and was designed to give business executives experiential insights into such matters as how leadership emerges in unstructured groups. Encounter groups got started more recently on the West Coast as part of the "human potential movement" and have close ties to such spawning grounds as Esalen Institute in Big Sur.

COGNITIVE BEHAVIOR MODIFICATION

If encounter groups revolve around immediate feelings, cognitive behavior modification treatments center upon immediate ideas. Whether we are talking about Aaron Beck's cognitive therapy for depression or Albert Ellis's rational-emotive methods, the emphasis is on replacing bad (dysfunctional) thoughts with good ones, on the assumption that what a person thinks potently affects what that person feels and does.[9, 10] The proverbial "man in the street," has always known this, of course, but many schools of psychology have given little attention to ideas, and some, such as militant behaviorism, have claimed that ideas are merely the passive by-products of overt actions.

It is one thing to fail an exam or not get promoted in the corporation, both of which are "facts." It is quite another thing, as Ellis has pointed out, to say to yourself that *because* something has happened you are worthless, terrible, and no good. The interpretive meanings we give to events are crucially important. Self-defeating statements, for example, "I can't do it" or "Nothing will ever go well for me," are psychologically toxic and, according to cognitive therapists, pathogenic. As the Palo Alto interaction theorists have suggested, how we "frame"—give meaning to—an incident has a lot to do with its psychological impact on us.[11]

This stress on patterns of thinking, if not taken so far as to make of reality a mere private construction to be manipulated at will, seems theologically reasonable. There is, after all, plenty of biblical material to support the hypothesis that ideas are very important.

That they are of critical significance in soteriological matters I do not dispute, as long as it is recognized that an "idea" in Scripture is not a cold abstraction but something closely related to the heart, to emotions and desires. It is more difficult to determine with any certainty how central a role ideas play in ordinary depressions, fears, conflicts, twitches, and family squabbles. Surely they are important. But *how* important? Even if ideas are uniquely important, there remains the question of how best to alter them. Perhaps a frontal assault, such as what often seems to happen in rational-emotive therapy, is not the most effective method, at least not for all people.

These comments notwithstanding, cognitive behavior modification approaches are on the rise. As long as the particular cognitive modifications do not fly in the face of the Christian view of life, there is no theological reason not to use them when they promise to ameliorate human suffering. In fact, under such circumstances, we have a duty to do so.

GESTALT THERAPY

Gestalt therapy was developed by "Fritz" Perls and several of his close associates.[12] *Gestalt* is the German word that roughly translates into English as "form" or "pattern." In Gestalt therapy, great emphasis is placed on expressing previously unexpressed aspects of oneself —especially feelings—and on "owning" those parts of oneself that one has come to disown. Beyond ameliorating symptoms of the usual sort, Gestalt procedures are designed to help people become more self-nourishing and independent.

In at least one respect, Gestalt therapy is the antithesis of cognitive behavior modification, which essentially involves conditioning people to think differently and, thus, to better manage their feelings and actions. According to the Gestaltist, too much such management is precisely the problem! The Gestalt therapist wants to enhance spontaneity, not shore up weakening walls of control. George Santayana, the twentieth-century Harvard philosopher, is known for his clever quips such as his comment to the effect that a fanatic is one who, having lost sight of his purpose, redoubles his efforts. The neurotic, in the view of the Gestalt therapist, acts out a similar pattern, blindly intensifying the very thing that made for all the trouble to begin with. Sensing his or her defenses to be faltering, the person in psychological difficulty attempts to strengthen them, often with the help of all kinds of popular and professional self-regulation techniques. "The neurotic wants, not to get rid of the neurosis, but to perfect it." In this quest, the Gestalt practitioner wants no part.

Gestalt methods include working with dreams. Sometimes this is done by having patients act them out in therapy, on the theory that each part of the dream stands for some unexpressed part of the personality. Another well-known Gestalt technique is having the patient portray dialogues. For example, two chairs will be placed opposite each other. The patient sits in one and puts someone else (or himself/herself) in the other. This may be a parent, a spouse, or a friend. As the client talks to the person in the other chair, the therapist may "feed" in appropriate sentences. Then the patient may be asked to switch chairs, to *be* the other person and to respond. In each chair, he or she is directed to attend carefully to voice quality, posture, breathing, and so on. Many other methods are also used by Gestalt clinicians who, in general, play down the use of canned techniques—gimmicks—in favor of the therapist creatively improvising, based on fully focused awareness.

An imposing theological problem arises from the philosophic rhetoric that often rides on the back of the formidable Gestalt stead. This rhetoric is one of individualism and is expressed in Perls's "Gestalt prayer," which begins "I do my thing and you do your thing." It goes on to say that we are not here to live up to others' expectations. Such a philosophy, if carried to extremes, fosters self-absorption and leaves little room for true community—for the kind of commitment to others embodied in the Gospels.

At the same time, I can appreciate why Perls voiced what sounds like a platform of narcissistic selfishness. He was responding to the unhealthy, sticky, manipulative, and symbiotic "togetherness" he often saw. Ironically, few groups are as cohesive as Gestalt therapists and their followers, which may substantially answer my criticism. On the clinical plane, I believe that competent Gestalt therapists help a great many people, mostly by loosening up their affects and encouraging them to "take responsibility" for themselves. Gestalt therapists attempt to "frustrate the neurosis." As long as they remain sensitive and halfway warm during the process, the treatment will probably be beneficial.

BODY-ORIENTED THERAPIES

For a variety of reasons too complex to address here, Gestalt therapists (and encounter group leaders) seem drawn to body-oriented therapies. These include bioenergetics, Rolfing, and various forms of "sensate focusing," sometimes with a bit of nutritional guidance thrown in. Usually the theory is that the body plays a key role in psychological troubles, since presumably it is the repository, the tangible memory bank, of psychic trauma. The theme of these approaches is, collectively, "unlock the body and you unlock the repressed feelings associated with the trauma."

This theme is not as offbeat as it may, at first, sound (although a large number of offbeat people get involved in it). There are too many reliable stories of powerful emotional reactions coming about through somatic methods to dismiss them out of hand. To become more aware of our bodies in all their subtleties, to *feel* ourselves from the inside and to have our physical structures aligned properly, seem manifestly valuable, quite aside from the questions of emotional release. Whether or not body therapies alone will "cure neurosis" I do not know.

What I do know is that a therapist's attitude of "get in touch with your body" often seems to go along with one of "get in touch with *my* body." It must be said in fairness, however, that sexual attitudes are not intrinsically related to most of the methods, which may be quite sound. The trick may be to find a somatic practitioner who sticks to the job of providing legitimate therapy and who has attitudes that, at least, do not conflict with Christian norms.

PSYCHOANALYSIS

Finally, we come to the grandparent of all psycho-therapeutic methods, psychoanalysis. It has been said that psychoanalysis is a theory of personality, a clinical research method, and a form of treatment. Our concern is with the last of these.

The biggest problem in trying to discuss psycho-analysis is that it has such a long and convoluted history that one can scarcely consider it a single thing. At root, the psychoanalytic method involves the analyst attempting to facilitate the patient's awareness of that which was previously repressed, hidden, unconscious.

This is done by the analyst making carefully timed interpretations of the analysand's free associations. The aim of the method, and the presumed vehicle of cure, has always been said to be "insight." It must be conceded, however, that when good psychoanalysts talk about insight, they are *not* referring to detached, emotionless intellectualizations.[13] A good analysis is anything but a casual process of stringing together egocentric conjectures as to the origins and natures of one's mental dynamics. To the contrary, it is a soul-wrenching battle for growth.

It has been fashionable for advocates of new therapies to use psychoanalysis as a foil, to treat it as a whipping boy. Often these advocates select for demonstration the lamest and most inept writings by analysts available. Psychoanalysts understandably take offense at this.

That analysis takes too long for the average not-too-troubled person to afford is undeniable. That it has been frequently weighted down with unnecessary theoretical baggage is true. That some analysts are cold, abstract, overly intellectual, and insufficiently oriented toward the experiencing and expressing of emotion is incontrovertible. That they are, on the whole, perhaps authoritarian instead of egalitarian may also be true, I do not know. Yet surely, when a school of therapy is as large and as old as psychoanalysis is, it is bound to be open to some criticism.

After years of reflection and training, much of it in institutions antagonistic to analytic theories and methods, I have had to conclude that a well-conducted psychoanalysis is still the best way by which to come to understand oneself. This does not mean, however, that it is always the best therapy. For one thing, as we suggested above, psychoanalysis is terribly expensive. If you have claustrophobia, you might do better to spend $500 on a behavior therapist than $50,000 on a psychoanalyst. But not all problems go away so easily; some people want more comprehensive treatment than the alleviation of a single symptom; and some people can and are willing to afford the long analytic process.

Sigmund Freud, the founder of psychoanalysis, is commonly presumed to be the archenemy of Christianity, owing perhaps to his views of sex and religion. Without belaboring the point, it is very much at issue whether Freud is any more problematic for Christianity than, say, Carl Jung or B. F. Skinner. It may be theologically more desirable to be viewed as a lustful creature who manufactures religion to meet his or her need for a loving father, than to be viewed as the passive product of a reinforcement history interacting with a collection of genes, totally determined by that history and those genes. Both Freud and Skinner are determinists, but Freud is a little less emphatic about it. As for Jung, who is often and mistakenly said to be the friend of Christianity, a close reading of his works will show that he never took it seriously *theologically* but simply co-opted it, in part, *psychologically.* Like Immanuel Kant, Jung thought that Christianity was useful.

This overview of psychotherapies has been, of necessity, brief. By devoting two chapters to it, we have managed to glance at the theological and clinical merits, and demerits, of a number of the more popular forms of psychological help currently in use. Anything resembling a comprehensive treatment of these therapies would run to a thousand pages. I am happy to say that a good friend of mine is writing an ethical analysis of modern psychotherapies, and another has completed a doctoral dissertation in a similar vein.[14, 15] What I have written here will, I hope, serve as a succinct guide to the real benefits, as well as the potential pitfalls, of the more common psychological approaches.

What is now in vogue as "therapy" may soon pass from the marketplace, only to be replaced by other helping procedures. Some of these will be genuine advances and some will be the psychological equivalents of sugar pills. Some may turn out to be, in the long run, destructive. Others will add to the rich resources available to the body of Christ.

Christians, and in particular Christian mental health professionals, must scrutinize carefully anything that is put forward as a psychological treatment. At this juncture in intellectual history it is clear that psychology is very much a discipline of fads and fashions. This carries with it the disadvantage of fickleness. It carries the great advantage, however, of innovation. An immense amount of creativity has been put into the hands of the church by the behavioral sciences. The church, to be true to its mission, cannot afford the ill-begotten luxury of sticking its head in the sand, either through refusing to avail itself of this creativity or through blindly appropriating every new psychological idea to come along.

In the next chapter I want to present some of my personal experiences of Christ *in* psychotherapy. Our Lord comes to us with many faces. Sometimes the face he wears is our closest friend's. Sometimes it is our husband's or wife's. Sometimes it is our therapist's.

NOTES
 1. Eric Berne, *Games People Play* (New York: Grove Press, 1964).
 2. For example, Thomas Harris, *I'm OK, You're OK* (New York: Harper & Row, 1967).
 3. For a recent statement of family therapy theory, see James L. Framo, "Family Theory and Therapy," *American Psychologist* 34 (1979): 988-992.
 4. Allen E. Bergin and Michael J. Lambert, "The Evaluation of Therapeutic Outcomes," in Sol L. Garfield and Allen E. Bergin (eds.), *Handbook of Psychotherapy and Behavior Change: An Empirical Analysis* (second ed.), 1978.
 5. Jean-Paul Sartre is well known for popularizing this phrase.
 6. Harry Stack Sullivan, *The Interpersonal Theory of Psychiatry* (New York: Norton, 1953).
 7. See Martin Lakin, *Interpersonal Encounter: Theory and Practice in Sensitivity Training* (New York: McGraw-Hill, 1972).
 8. See Berne, *Games People Play*, p. 124.
 9. Aaron T. Back, *Cognitive Therapy and the Emotional Disorders* (New York: International Universities Press, 1976).
10. Albert Ellis, *Reason and Emotion in Psychotherapy* (New York: Lyle Stuart, 1962).
11. For example, Paul Watzlawick, *How Real Is Real?* (New York: Random House, 1976).

12. Frederick Perls, *Gestalt Therapy Verbatim* (Lafayette, Cal.: Real People Press, 1969).

13. For an overview of psychoanalytic technique, see Charles Brenner, *Psychoanalytic Technique and Psychic Conflict* (New York: International Universities Press, 1976).

14. Donald Miller, professor at the University of Southern California, is currently writing a book on this topic.

15. Beverly Hagner just completed a dissertation in which she draws out the ethical implications of several popular therapy systems.

ELEVEN
CHRIST IN PSYCHOTHERAPY

"I am God Almighty. Live always in my presence." This was the instruction given to the aged Abram, on the eve of the Lord establishing through him the spiritual and national entity known as Israel (Genesis 17:1, NEB). Is this not a curious command? If God is omnipresent, how could anyone *not* live in his presence? Looking back through the long tunnel of history, it is clear that "live always in my presence" is a *psychological* imperative.

An atheist is one who does not acknowledge God's existence. Abram is being told, "Live in the awareness that I am." Since to be aware that *God* exists implies that one is aware of at least the rudimentary outline of God's nature and the general ordering of things, Abram is being told, "Live in relationship to me—God, the Creator and Provider." He is being told, in essence, to bear in mind his own creatureliness (see Romans 1) and not to live as an atheist. In this chapter, I want to discuss what psychotherapy may have to do with living in God's presence.

Since I wrote the early drafts of this book manuscript, I have had two personal experiences of Christ in psychotherapy, one formal, the other informal. When I wrote these first drafts, I had never been to a Christian therapist! I was a Christian therapist, and I had consulted other therapists here and there along the way, but I had never been the client of anyone I could be assured was a Christian. If one is going to write about Christ and psychotherapy, one ought to have experienced Christ *in* therapy, or perhaps I should say *through* therapy, indeed through the therapist. For some things, there is just no substitute for experiential knowledge. In studying Christ in psychotherapy, perhaps the most valid perspective of all is the one through the patient's eye.

Some Unorthodox Orthodoxy. Several years ago, another psychologist and I decided that we would exchange "informal" hours. She would see me every other Tuesday at 2:00, and I would see her on the alternate Tuesdays. This sort of thing is not supposed to work, and almost any psychologist will tell you that it runs counter to how the healing process is ordinarily assumed to operate. But it worked admirably. (While this colleague is quick to reassure me, I rather think that I got more out of the process than she did—I had the greater need!)

While the "body of Christ" is in some sense mystical, it is more than a metaphor. When I poured out my pains and struggles to this beloved colleague and saw the tears run down her face, I saw Jesus Christ. In these moments she was Christ to me.

This is at times a sobering realization, since it seems to place an eternal, and by implication an infinitely valuable, premium on all human interactions. There is both an awesome power and an almost unfathomable responsibility in this reality.

What was it about our encounters that I found so healing, so Christian and, in the final tally, so radically different? Some of this difference may be attributable to good human chemistry—she and I might have "clicked" under any circumstances, quite aside from our faith or the lack of it. Some of the difference may simply indicate that she is a very skilled psychologist. But I believe there is more to it than this. As best I can determine, here are the active ingredients in the "treatment" she provided for me:

First, I was absolutely convinced that she genuinely loved me as I was, frailties and all. The idea of genuinely loving a patient puts together two Rogerian ideas (see chapter 9), authenticity (congruence) and nonpossessive warmth (unconditional positive regard)—in other words, honest caring. I have seen many therapists stumble over the terrain where warmth and genuineness are supposed to intersect. What do you do when, in fact, you do *not* feel truly accepting toward a client? Do you fake the warmth, or reject the client? I believe that her ability to accept and affirm me reflected Christ's love. Through her eyes she radiated the Master.

Second, she showed that she could feel. She was not afraid to care. Few experiences in life are more toxic than consulting a "technician." No matter how well trained, no matter how full of therapeutic ideas and procedures, technicians do not meet you where you are. Words of understanding, regardless of how expertly crafted, become meaningless if not backed up with the message, "I feel it as you feel it." This is the third Rogerian quality, empathy. Representing Christ to me, she felt it as *I* felt it.

Third, she communicated integrity. This, to me, meant more than simple honesty, although it certainly included that. It implied courage, a willingness to say and do what others may not like. Sometimes the "other" was me. This colleague and I are very close friends, but that did not stop her a bit! Like it or not, she told me the truth. At the same time she was always gentle and patient. She "spoke the truth in love" (Ephesians 4:15, NEB). Never did I have the sense that she was confronting me for her sake, say to work out her frustrations. Also, I had the deep assurance that, no matter what, she would not subordinate my welfare to hers. Here, once again, we find the enigmatic intertwining of the spiritual and the psychological. What a therapist *does* reflects who he or she *is*.

Fourth, her core beliefs and values were manifestly

Christian. They were, therefore, in accord with the infrastructure of life, with the ontological and ethical groundwork of the universe. Although she and I differed on specific issues, I knew that she deeply embraced the divinity of Christ, that she was concerned about her own spiritual welfare as well as mine, and that she prayed for both of us. The often unspoken backdrop to everything we did together was a shared awareness that the Lord, God Almighty, was calling *us* to live in his presence. She and I knew in whom our ultimate salvation lay. Yet, during our times together, there was nothing that smacked of "religion in the service of defenses," of trying to avoid distressing thoughts and feelings by clinging to empty religious language. Such references as she made to God were deeply meaningful to both of us. They were sincere and they were reverent. They communicated the fact that when she referred to God, she knew there was a God. My awareness of her faith on many occasions nourished my own.

The fifth quality I believe to have been of great benefit was her clear professional competence. On the surface, there seems to be nothing particularly Christian about this. Many unbelieving practitioners are competent; in fact, I know a good number of avowed agnostic therapists to whom I would rather refer clients than to some of the Christian professionals I know. However, if God is the Source of all good, regardless of who does it, there is something Christian about competence after all. Moreover, I strongly believe that her Christlike love for people is largely what has motivated her to develop her clinical expertise.

We must now address directly the question of the Christian therapist's pastoral responsibilities.[1] There is always the possibility that therapy will fall far short of what it ideally could be, through the failure of the Christian clinician to integrate proper spiritual concerns into the healing process. As Jerome Frank points out, people who consult therapists are usually demoralized.[2] In my view, they are often looking for theological-philosophical answers as much as anything else. To take the edge off someone's despair without at least nodding in the direction of Christ may be, in the long run, to do that person a serious disservice.

It is both unworkable and unrealistic to attempt to dodge the problem of how to integrate Christianity and psychotherapy by simply ignoring it, or by rigidly compartmentalizing the religious and metaphysical on one hand from the psychological and physical on the other. In practice, these *cannot* be neatly separated. The mere fact that clients frequently go to great lengths to find out about the personal beliefs and practices of their therapists is in itself enough to alert any thinking practitioner to the need for "integration," or at very least to the need for addressing philosophical questions. My colleague Phyllis Hart addressed them in a thousand ways, through well over a hundred hours that I spent in her consulting office.

Coming to Terms with God and Self. The second of my personal therapeutic experiences reflects the ongoing courageous attempt by a psychologist to face these questions. John Finch, who calls his approach "Christian Existential Psychotherapy," explicitly intends his treatment procedures to enhance the client's spirituality.[3]

The particular procedure for which he is best known is called "Intensive Therapy." It takes three weeks. During this time, the client lives alone in one of several secluded houses set aside expressly for intensive patients. No phone calls, no letters, no reading . . . nothing that would distract one from the treatment. Except for the weekend between the second and third weeks, during which the client is allowed to reenter the labyrinths of society, these long days of seclusion are punctuated only by a daily, early morning drive to and from the therapy hour. I went for Intensive Therapy in January of 1980.

"No [person] is worthy of me who cares more for father or mother. . . . By gaining his life a man will lose it" (Matthew 10:37-39, NEB). It looks as if Jesus is saying,

"You can't be my disciple if you let your loyalties to family supersede your loyalty to me, and neither can you be mine if you are a coward, afraid to put your life on the line." These interpretations may be valid, but I think there is a deeper meaning in the passage. I would render it something like this: "If you are still so preoccupied with gaining the love of your mother or father that you cannot truly love me, you will not be able to walk with me." Further, "Holding on to psycho-spiritual illusions will ultimately destroy you." Intensive Therapy is designed to help patients give up such illusions.

The scriptural passage above has to do with what has been called the "struggle" and the "unreal self." While I do not want to convey the idea that to be a Christian one has to be prepared by the psychotherapist, it does seem that we are now considering a domain of existence where sin and neurosis genuinely intersect—a true point of integration.

The struggle is the potentially endless attempt to win a mother and father's love, as well as the defensive effort to keep alive one's hope of doing so. The unreal self is the set of performances we put on, for ourselves and others, to keep us from feeling the pain within. According to the theory undergirding Intensive Therapy, there is no end to the struggle, or to the suffering that goes along with it, until this pain is experienced in all its horror. This is so because the struggle is a symbolic one, a quest for that which *cannot* satisfy us, since what we really seek is love from actual human beings, who may be unwilling or unable to give it. Even if our parents are alive and were now to give us what we have always wanted, they cannot give love to the child who needed it "then." Suffering comes from the continual frustration of finding that symbolic achievements do not create lasting satisfaction. It also comes from stiffening ourselves against the pain, and against the seemingly terrible realization that we will never be loved *as a child* "back then." Coming to terms with this horrible reality is central to the intensive procedure.

Arthur Janov wrote, "the more pain we feel, the less pain we suffer."[4] He was saying that we can put an end to neurotic suffering only to the degree that we face our agonies, that we *experience* the sadness and pain of not being fully loved. Well-conducted psychotherapy can help people confront their hurts, and thus can help them end the neurotic struggle—"neurotic" because it does not work and, moreover, gets compulsively repeated over and over again. It seems evident that to give up the struggle is spiritually profitable, at least to the extent that we resolve the feelings that motivated it and are pointed to God in the process. To stop running from the emptiness is to reckon with this emptiness, which is potentially to open ourselves up to God.

"Clinton, this is for you. Get everything you can out of it. When else in your life will you get three weeks for yourself, just for you?" With these words, Dr. Finch left me at 6:00 P.M. before my Intensive began. For the next twenty days, I would do little except feel, write down what I felt, and keep my therapy appointment every morning at 7:00.

Doing "nothing" is not easy for me. My whole life has been filled with activity and movement. What I found out through the experience is that, by refusing to engage in one's typical activities and movements, one is left alone to encounter the universe with little defense. It is to become anxious. It is to risk feeling oneself, in all of one's previously unexpressed desperation.

Regardless of the form of one's particular struggle —striving to be popular, working to earn more money, making sure never to get anyone else angry, seeking professional stature, climbing the corporate ladder, getting more than enough sex, fishing endlessly for reassurances, and so on—the struggle takes energy. It impairs our happiness and our relationship with God. No experience in life is quite like crying out to the heavens, "Okay, I give up! It's no use struggling anymore. I see that now. Lord, I give you my life (once again)."

I said words to this effect from the waterfront porch of the seclusion house. "Live always in my presence."

By encountering one's aloneness—facing what John Finch and others call the "abyss" and not masking it with Band-Aids of diversion—one confronts the *void* that only God can fill.

Among the ideas informing Finch's treatment is a concept of duty. "To be a whole person to each moment and incident" is part of this concept. Once again, no matter how hard we may try to keep health and holiness separate from each other, sooner or later they stand face to face. Psychological and religious issues can only be kept separate for so long without damage to everyone.

There is, for example, a subtle interpenetration of defensiveness and dishonesty. At times, it is almost as if these are different words for the same thing—terms from two different domains of discourse, the moral and the psychological. Defenses, in the Freudian scheme, are said to operate unconsciously. Yet the line between conscious and unconscious is every bit as fuzzy as the one between the moral and the psychological. Surely there must be *some* volitional aspect to defenses. At the same time, much of what seems like moral, or immoral, behavior probably operates reflexively, without much intention behind it. A psychological construct like "defense mechanism" takes the "moralism" out of the matter, leaving judgment appropriately to God as the only true Judge of the human heart. Still, the point remains that there is some connection, however ambiguous, between the spiritual and the psychological. Life is as fascinating as it is partly because of our inability to identify, in most instances, the extent to which people are truly responsible for what they do. Only God can see "inside." We are forever stuck with an outsider's perspective of another person's mind, heart, and spirit.

One way to avoid coming to terms with this ambiguous convergence of the spiritual and the psychological is to adopt a secular conception of mental health that simply ignores or explains away the religious. As I suggested in an earlier chapter, most clinicians adopt some version of the view that mental well-being is freedom from excess anxiety, maintaining good relationships, having accurate perspectives of reality, etc.

One cannot really adopt such a view while insisting that a person must be a Christian to be healthy, since this insistence modifies the standard view. Furthermore, as we saw, one cannot equate health and holiness without altering the usual meanings of these terms. Perhaps we need to *expand* these customary meanings. It may be manifestly imprudent to lop off from clinical psychology, and its sister disciplines, so large and vital an area of human functioning as the spiritual. To be "whole" may mean a good deal more than the absence of symptoms. It may mean living in relationship with the Creator. It may mean to see with spiritual eyes, to feel with a warm and grateful heart, and to love other people.

Psychologists have continually lamented the absence of what is termed a positive view of mental health, a definition that says what it *is* and not just what it is not (e.g., freedom from overt psychopathology). Perhaps it is time for Christian psychologists to rise to the challenge. Our fears, of the state and of our colleagues, may tempt us to shrink back from such an effort, but it may be that to shirk our duty to this "moment and incident" in history is to miserably fail ourselves, our world, and our God. Psychotherapy, rightly understood and practiced, may come to much more than deconditioning fears, improving social relationships, generating psychodynamic insights, or even providing genuine warmth and empathy. By the sheer weight of the psychotherapeutic situation—hurting people looking not just for symptom relief but also for growth and existential guidance—the psychotherapist may not have the option of refusing to be an existential guide. Implicitly or explicitly, the therapist will probably either point people toward God, or nudge them in some other direction. There may be no neutrality in the end.

I find the experience of writing this distressing, yet at the same time exhilarating. As professionally awkward as it may turn out to be, the call for Christian therapists to *be* Christ to their patients must be taken seriously.

At the risk of being two self-disclosing, I want to say something about what I got out of Intensive Therapy. As I intimated above, I have lived a very active life, a life in which achievement has been centrally important. During my first week with him, John remarked almost casually, "You are rather driven, you know." We worked on and around this theme for most of my time in Washington.

In the time since my Intensive, I have discovered the most remarkable thing about myself. In a word, much of my ambition is gone, or perhaps I should say my "ambitiousness." While I work as hard, for the most part, as I always have, the experience of working for me now is much lighter, much more filled with joy. Much of the compulsion is gone. I do not *need* achievement anymore (though I still value it highly). Whether this sense of freedom will last, I do not know, but it feels very good, very good indeed.

Therapy Beyond the Office. Before ending this personal chapter, I would like to suggest that all therapy does not happen in a doctor's office. To be sure, some of the best psychotherapy occurs between friends over coffee.

For well over a decade, I have shared my triumphs and defeats, my agonies and ecstasies with several close friends who are not psychologists. Each of them has given me a great deal of help, and I would not hesitate to call some of it psychotherapy. In these relationships there is commitment, concern, camaraderie. Most of all, there is Christ. I *see* Christ in these friends, as the acknowledgments at the front of this book certify.

Two years ago, I joined a morning prayer and fellowship group started by a close friend. The seven people in this group all attend First Presbyterian Church of Hollywood. Besides me, there are two attorneys, an architect, a minister, a musical conductor, and a manufacturer. To our mutual delight, the sharing that goes on in our group is often very deep and very meaningful. Here is help, vital help, from within the body of Christ. Indeed, for me the group has provided what I would call rich psychotherapeutic help!

A new age in the church may be dawning, an age of openness, caring, and nonjudgmental compassion. Our group is perhaps one expression of this new age. In it people take risks. They also honor others' risks and keep their confidences. Whereas above I wrote of Christ in formal psychotherapy, this group and my other close friendships reflect Christ in informal psychotherapy.

I would like to reiterate that the church cannot afford to disregard the resources of the mental health professions. When and where appropriate, these resources must be worked into the warp and woof of caring within the church universal, as it often is in my fellowship group. While at times the church has regarded psychology as its enemy, the psychologist is no more the necessary enemy of Christ than the biologist. It is only the religious beliefs, or unbeliefs, of individual scientists or practitioners that are problematic.

What did the church and the rest of the world do with "psychopathology" before the emergence of psychology and psychiatry? The same thing it did with malaria, small pox, and polio before their cures were discovered. It was forced to leave them to inflict their miseries on living, breathing, feeling human beings. Uncle Harry, as well as the little child next door—the one with the innocent eyes and the cherubic face —suffered and frequently died. At this juncture in history, those of us in the church have a choice.

The only reasonable option we have is to learn everything we can from psychologists, psychiatrists, social workers, and every other group of legitimate mental health practitioners. The church must take them in, not cast them out. It is my conviction that every significant, health-producing relationship I have is informed, to some extent, by the wisdom of the behavioral sciences. It is the therapists who have most addressed the need for self-disclosure, for emotional dialogue, for intelligent compassion. They have done what the church is charged to do—care effectively for people. Society needs Christians who are therapists, therapists who will radiate to it the light of Jesus Christ, Son of God, Redeemer of the World. If Christ *is* the Way, the Truth, and the *Life,* people at this point in history may need to be told so, particularly by members of the psychological professions.

NOTES

1. For an example of a theorist who, in essence, does not distinguish between pastoral counseling and psychotherapy, see Gary R. Collins, *The Rebuilding of Psychology: Toward an Integration of Psychology and Christianity* (Wheaton, Ill.: Tyndale, 1977).

2. See Jerome Frank, *Persuasion and Healing* (Baltimore: Johns Hopkins University Press, 1961).

3. H. Newton Malony, Professor of Psychology and Director of Programs in Integration at Fuller Theological Seminary, has edited a book of contributions by John G. Finch.

4. Arthur Janov, *The Primal Scream* (New York: Dell, 1970).

TWELVE
LOOKING BACKWARD
AND FORWARD

A new era is dawning, an era in which the emotional
hurts of people may be given something like the
attention that God has wanted them to have all along.
Christians are beginning to rid themselves of pretense,
perfectionism, and pride. It is becoming acceptable for
us to admit to each other that we are not always on top
of things, that we ache from time to time, and that sin
in its many forms—not just our sin but the fallen nature
of the world—has cut deeply into the fabric of our
personalities. We are learning that people cannot love
us if they do not know us.[1] They can bind only the
wounds they know about.

An increasing number of Christian psychologists are
putting their time and energy into thinking through the
sorts of issues we have considered. These psychologists
are not content to view psychotherapy and Christianity
as two unrelated enterprises. Books are being written.
Articles are being published. Talks are being given.

I have tried in this book to clear away the intellectual
underbrush. Specifically, I have pointed out the key
metaphysical, epistemological, and ethical issues that
emerge as one tries to integrate psychotherapy with the
Christian world view. In doing this, I have regarded
psychotherapy as an art informed by the science of

empirical psychology, and I have taken pains to note the difference between philosophic and scientific questions. Questions about the ontological nature of humanity, the moral worth of particular human actions, the meaning of life, the validity of religious truth claims, or the path of salvation and eternal life are not answerable by science—they never have been and they never will be.

We have also briefly examined New Testament writings to see what they have to say about human personality, surveyed popular psychotherapeutic methods, and explored the importance of the mystical to human living and, by implication, to psychotherapy. We have, in addition, explored the relationship between emotional healing and regeneration, the ethics of a therapist telling a client about the person and work of Jesus Christ, and the relationship between health and law. I have also shared some of my personal experiences of Christ in psychotherapy. It might be helpful at this point to review some of the positions that I have argued:

1. How we define psychological health is extremely important. It is possible for an individual to be a paragon of mental health, as this is traditionally defined, and yet be living without faith in God through Christ. Indeed, such a person might claim to be an ardent atheist. Health in its usual sense, therefore, cannot be taken as *de facto* evidence of Christian regeneration. It may be appropriate for Christian psychotherapists to develop their own conceptions of psychological well-being, conceptions that include considerations of faith.

2. Turning the issue around, the presence of psychological problems in someone's life does not invalidate, or even cast doubt, on his or her Christianity. All of us have problems. We are fallen creatures living on a fallen planet. While we can reasonably expect Christianity to enhance a person's psychological well-being, we cannot expect Christians to be psychologically perfect. The doctrine of sin, in fact, implies the utter impossibility of perfection. Since we can never tell with certainty what "raw material" a

person brought with him or her *to* Christianity, we have no reliable standard against which to measure *anyone's* growth—except our own. This is why we are told not to judge others.

3. Keeping the Law does *not* always seem to enhance temporal psychological well-being. Certain persons in certain situations seem to face the cruel dilemma of having to choose between two kinds of "goods." Stated differently, ultimate and temporal good are not always correspondent and, at times, they *may* be inversely related. While there is debate over whether God wants people in such circumstances to break his Law, God surely rejoices over human growth however it comes about. He loves us as ends in ourselves. Were we living in the Garden of Eden before the Fall, there would be no disparity between ultimate and penultimate good. However, since sin is fibrously woven into the universe, we sometimes face excruciatingly hard moral choices. Just about everything in this life is some ambiguous mixture of good and bad, which is what makes these choices so difficult.

4. Psychotherapy, if successful, will help a person feel and act better. In this sense, it will enhance what Lewis called "nearness of likeness" to God. This will be true even if both the therapist and the client are avowed atheists. It will also be true if the client is a Christian but the therapist is not. "Nearness of likeness," however, must not be confused with "nearness of approach." Feeling and acting better may or may not help a person move closer to God. Upon occasion it may even retard such movement, since it may take the edge off healthy despair—the kind of despair that leads to repentance and surrender. As mortal beings, though, we can never identify these "occasions" with any sort of certainty. Consequently, with Jesus as our model, Christian therapists should bring emotional healing to anyone they can.

5. The practice of psychotherapy, by itself, must not be confused with Christian evangelism, unless of course this practice includes reference to the saving work of

Christ. Such reference may in some instances consist of little more than the therapist giving the client a book (such as C. S. Lewis's *Mere Christianity*, or John Stott's *Basic Christianity*). If it is true that all persons need to know about Christ's person and work, Christian therapists may be defaulting on an opportunity and a crucial responsibility if they fail to share the gospel with their clients (presumably Christian plumbers, lawyers, and businesspersons share the gospel with *their* clients). It can, of course, be argued that evangelism is a distinct function to be carried on by a distinct arm of the church and that neither therapists, plumbers, lawyers, nor businesspeople should be expected to share their faith in the course of their work. Regardless of how an individual Christian resolves this particular question, it is crucial to keep in mind the simple fact that evangelism involves explicit reference to sin, the nature of regeneration, and God's provision for our salvation.

6. All reputable forms of psychotherapy probably have something valuable to offer, and so it is best to remain open to all of them. Psychotherapy is, at root, self-disclosure to a wise and understanding advisor. Sometimes this advice comes in the form of interpretations as to what this or that means (e.g., in psychoanalysis). Sometimes it consists of recommendations as to how one should act to achieve a desired result (e.g., in behavior therapy). This list is theoretically endless. Christians should become good shoppers of psychological services, choosing them on the basis of specific needs.

7. The Bible contains no scientific theory of personality. Paul's "psychology" of the person addresses metaphysical and ethical questions more than questions of everyday intrapsychic functioning. Clinical information, such as any competent psychotherapist knows and uses, simply does not appear in Scripture. At the same time, both Christian practitioners and psychotherapy clients should be alert to the possibility of alien philosophic notions slipping in the back door

of the consulting room. Science is science and philosophy is philosophy. One should not be panned off as the other.

8. Complex ethical dilemmas surround the matter of introducing Christian witness into the psychotherapy hour. It may turn out that the therapist is always advocating *some* kind of religion (in the broad sense), whether Christianity or humanism. If this is so, the Christian therapist may truly be caught between the state and the church. In a permissive society such as ours, the best course of action may be "truth in packaging." Much has been written of late on "informed consent," the notion that consumers of psychological services should be told *in advance* what will be done with and to them. All therapists ought to tell prospective clients about their professional qualifications and orientations, and about their personal beliefs.

9. Moral decisions should be left to the client. When a therapist, especially a Christian therapist, perceives that a client has to make one of those cruel ethical decisions referred to above, the therapist should say, to the best of his or her ability, what outcomes are likely to attend each alternative. Christian therapists treating other Christians need to be particularly careful to communicate grace and acceptance rather than Law and judgment. At the same time, I believe that a therapist is going beyond the limits of propriety if he or she advocates breaking the Law. It has been argued by some that certain clients are too weak and emotionally disabled to make their own ethical decisions. The Christian therapist needs to be alert to the possibility that this may be nothing more than a way to manipulate the therapist into assuming too much responsibility.

10. Modern psychology and psychotherapy are truly new, just as the physics of subatomic particles is new. They were simply not available to first-century Christians. The church stands in a position to profit immensely from psychology, which should not be viewed as an enemy. To the contrary, we should embrace it,

make it our own, and lead the way to its further development. Also, Christian psychotherapists must take seriously the nature of the human spirit. It may not be possible, after all, to treat a client for an extended period of time without getting into matters of a spiritual nature. The church needs psychology and psychology needs the church. The times are exciting, the possibilities enormous.

NOTE

1. The idea that you can only love people if you know them came from Phyllis Hart. She further maintains that intimacy between persons is inextricably tied up with *agape*, indeed with what the body of Christ is to be.

A SHORT POSTSCRIPT ON SIN

Sin is the terrible disease that afflicts all persons. If we weren't sinners, there would be no need for redemption and regeneration, and consequently Jesus Christ would have died as an ill-fated martyr. But what precisely is sin, and what does it mean to be a sinner?

There are at least two ways to define sin, and for years I thought that one had to choose between them. There is sin as doing what one knows to be wrong, and there is sin as doing wrong, quite aside from whether or not one knows it. According to the first conception, something is sin *only* if the person understands that it is wrong. According to the second conception, which is much broader, *anything* that runs counter to God's perfect will is inherently sin. The exegesis of sin as "missing the mark" supports the latter view, which implies that we are accountable for our behavior, no matter what—"ignorance is no excuse in the eyes of the law."

In the hope of shedding light on the nature of sin, and to illustrate how difficult it is to evaluate the culpability of a person who commits a particular sin, I offer this conception:

Sin is, at root, the failure to be what God intends us to be. The extent to which any one thing is sinful (full of sin), however, depends on two other things. These are awareness and capacity.

Someone who does something in the full knowledge that it is wrong but who has very little capacity to resist (*A*) may be about as culpable as someone who does something he or she could easily resist but which he or she does not know to be wrong (*B*). An example of the first situation would be a person who, because of a brain tumor, acts violently but who has deep remorse. An example of the second situation would be a headhunter who has so much tribal standing that he has no need of collecting more heads. He can easily refrain from another murder, but he would be unlikely to regard such a murder as radically wrong.

The person who has both clear knowledge of the wrongness of something and total capacity to refrain from it is the most culpable of all (*C*), while a person who neither knows nor can resist is perhaps least culpable (*D*)—least sin-full. A well-adjusted Christian who premeditatedly offends someone, therefore, may be far more sinful than a homicidal aborigine. "To whom much is given, much will be required."

All of us, in the face of every act, have some indeterminate measure of moral awareness *and* moral capacity. Both of these are strongly conditioned by our life experiences, however fortunate or unfortunate. God, I believe, takes both into account in judging our hearts. Thus, while we may be able to say that a particular act is wrong, we can never with certainty judge sinfulness, for sinfulness is an attribute of a person and not of what a person does, however heinous. Once again, we cannot judge on appearances, and since appearances are all we ever have, we should not judge persons at all.

A THEOLOGICAL RESPONSE
by Geoffrey W. Bromiley

Geoffrey W. Bromiley is perhaps the greatest living evangelical theologian. When this book was in the form of an earlier draft, I asked Bromiley to respond to it with a critical eye. What follows is what he wrote. While I would like to believe that the version of Scandal *that you hold in your hands is not vulnerable to some of his earlier criticisms, I will let you, the reader, decide! C.W.M.*

This book is to be welcomed as part of an ongoing attempt to study the relations between the sacred science of theology and the secular discipline of psychology. Because both theology and psychology are not just theoretical but highly practical as well, the investigation embraces a wide field and obviously has more than academic significance. This is especially true in view of the overlapping of the disciplines at many points. Since the same applies to the other social sciences, this type of study can also have the value of a spur or model or parallel for similar inquiries in other fields.

The overlapping can be an invitation to shortcutting, but Dr. McLemore wisely has not fallen into this trap. Perhaps the primary value of his work, and its most persistent theme, is to be found in the careful distinction he draws between psychology and theology—a distinction on which alone their true relation can be established. If the early chapters portray the distinction in principle, the chapters that follow offer working illustrations.

An important element in this clearing of the ground is the recognition of the validity of both a theological and a psychological approach. Only too easily differentiation might result in the arrogance which academic disciplines display when, perceiving differences of content and methodology in others, they either dismiss them out of hand or try to adjust or assimilate them to themselves. Here again the author has judiciously resisted temptation and argued that each of the sciences is valid in its own right and with its own terms of reference. As a psychologist himself, he has not assigned theology to a nonscientific corner nor tried to absorb it into his own sphere in the form of religious sociology.

Once the site is cleared, the possibility of reconstruction of the relation arises. Intentionally, in the present book, Dr. McLemore has not committed himself to this venture except by way of hints and intimations. Yet certain tasks seem to be suggested which it is to be hoped that he and others, perhaps in the form of monographs, will take in hand in the not-too-distant future. Thus a more precise understanding of theology is needed in which it is not so readily associated with the metaphysical and mystical but specifically related to the empirical data of the divine self-revelation in event as well as Scripture. Again the implications of the doctrine of creation need further study, partly along the lines of the author's reference to common grace, but also in relation to anthropology in all its aspects. A point here—and one of particular delicacy—is the indissolubility of divine and human relations which theology approaches from one angle and psychology from another but in which they necessarily encounter and may only too easily confront one another. Since both divine and human relations exist and are studied in